If These **WALLS** *Could* **TALK:**
CHICAGO BULLS

If These WALLS *Could* TALK:

CHICAGO BULLS

Stories from the
Sideline, Locker Room,
and Press Box of the
Chicago Bulls Dynasty

Kent McDill

TRIUMPH
B O O K S

Copyright © 2014 by Kent McDill

No part of this publication may be reproduced, stored in a retrieval system, or
transmitted in any form by any means, electronic, mechanical, photocopying,
or otherwise, without the prior written permission of the publisher, Triumph
Books LLC, 814 North Franklin Street, Chicago, Illinois 60610.

This book is available in quantity at special discounts for your group or
organization. For further information, contact:

Triumph Books LLC
814 North Franklin Street
Chicago, Illinois 60610
(312) 939-3330
www.triumphbooks.com

Printed in U.S.A.

ISBN: 978-1-60078-930-4

Design by Amy Carter

Photos courtesy of AP Images unless otherwise indicated

This book is dedicated to my wife, Janice, who kept our four children—Haley, Dan, Lindsey, and Kyle—alive and well while I was traveling with the Bulls.

CONTENTS

Foreword *by Bill Cartwright*   ix
Introduction   1
1. First Days   5
2. Bowling   8
3. The Most Amazing Jordan
   Story of Them All   9
4. 108–101 Win Over Lakers
   Brings First NBA Title Home   13
5. Me and Michael Jordan   16
6. Scottie Pippen   18
7. MVP   21
8. The Multiplex   24
9. What Scares Michael Jordan   26
10. Traveling   27
11. Jerry Krause   31
12. The First Championship
    Locker Room   37
13. Famous Reporters   41
14. Vegas   43
15. Drinking With Jordan   46
16. Twice Quite Nice for Bulls   52
17. Michael Jordan and the Kids   55
18. The Second Championship   60
19. Shoes   63
20. My Best Day Ever   65
21. The Phone Call   67

22. Playing the Game   68
23. On Top of the Game   72
24. Horace   75
25. The Twins   78
26. The Third Championship   79
27. My First and Only
    Practical Joke   81
28. Third Title Is In the Books   85
29. Jordan and Cartwright   88
30. Finally, Jordan Can Just
    Be Mike   90
31. Pippen's Hall of Fame Status   93
32. Michael Jordan Returns   94
33. Jordan Makes a Joke   97
34. Staying Alive in Miami   98
35. Dennis Rodman   101
36. Michael Jordan's Wallet   106
37. Autographs   106
38. Luc Longley   108
39. The National Anthem   111
40. Toni Kukoc   115
41. The Ron Harper Story   116
42. Home Indeed Proves
    to be Sweet   119
43. Pippen Calls His Shot   122
44. Jackson   123

45. He Went To Paris 126
46. Rodman Plays Basketball 132
47. Jordan Gets Older 135
48. Dennis Rodman Party 136
49. Jordan's Gambling 138
50. The Famous People I Met, and the One I Didn't 142
51. Technical Details 146
52. Clincher by Kerr, MJ's 39 Oust Jazz 151
53. When Athletes Asked Questions 154
54. My Biggest Bulls Story 156
55. Size Matters 162
56. "You Think You're Smart Because You Know Words" 164
57. NBA All-Star Game 167
58. Foreign Influences 172
59. Benny the Bull 176
60. MJ Closes the Deal Again 178
61. I Hated You! 182
62. Bird and Johnson 185
63. Jackson Wanted Rockets 189
64. An Indication of Just How Stupid I Am? 192
65. Freelance Gigs 195
66. Jordan Loves History 199
67. Injuries 201
68. A Bond with Sports That Lasted a Lifetime 206
69. Throwing Chairs 209
70. Comparing Incomparables 213
71. This Is the End 216
Acknowledgments 223

There's an old saying that "timing is everything in life." Often our choices are considered either good or bad based on timing alone. Whether you're telling a joke, cooking a soufflé, or shooting a basketball, what's the key ingredient?

Timing.

When Kent asked me to write the foreword for his book, I reflected on how perfect my timing was to be a part of the Bulls. I was the right age and had the right hunger to be a part of something special.

I was 31, and after playing for the New York Knicks for nine grueling years I was ready for a change. New York tests a professional athlete's character. New Yorkers are generally tough, worldly, and have an urban attitude. They voice their opinion whether asked for it or not. New Yorkers are simply critics, especially in sports.

The media reflected and fueled that mindset. You either found yourself on top of the world or on the back page of the *Post* under the headline "Trade Him." The writers could be downright despicable. Their goal was to put you down and look for anything and everything negative.

So it was a breath of fresh air when I went to Hawaii on vacation after the 1987–88 season and got a call from Jerry Krause, the general manager of the Chicago Bulls, who informed me that I'd been traded. My wife and I are from Sacramento, and the Midwest was more familiar territory than the East Coast, so we had renewed hope that Chicago could deliver everything New York could not.

Within hours, the Bulls brass was picking me up at the airport and—interestingly enough—took me to the Knickerbocker Hotel to meet Jerry. We talked about the team and my role. Being an elder statesman on the team, I would be one of its leaders.

I soon met the Chicago media, including a young Kent McDill. My nine seasons in New York had made me wary of sportswriters, but

I quickly found Kent and his cohorts were there to simply report on the happenings of the Bulls. They were more helpful than hurtful; their questions mostly concerned the team and where I fit in.

We had what would become our core group: Scottie Pippen, Horace Grant, Michael Jordan, John Paxson, and me. Our bench featured Sam Vincent, Craig Hodges, Charles Davis, Brad Sellers, and Dave Corzine. Our head coach Doug Collins had a great coaching staff. Collins, Johnny Bach, Tex Winter, Phil Jackson, and Jim Cleamons brought many years of basketball knowledge and creativity.

Doug loved veteran players and he welcomed me to do whatever I felt was best.

On the court and off, Chicago was a much better fit than New York had been for my family and me. We enjoyed the Art Institute, Field Museum, Lincoln Park Zoo, McCormick Place, the Shedd Aquarium and Oceanarium. And the people. They're courteous but their attitude is one of standing up for yourself—I won't push you if you don't push me.

That attitude informed the sports coverage. All players have a love-hate relationship with sportswriters. In Chicago the sportswriters want the same thing as the New York sportswriters; they want to write a sensational story that will interest readers and draw them in. I don't know if Chicago sportswriters are more caring than the New York sportswriters but they are more responsible—especially the beat writers.

Kent was one of the beat writers who was with the team on all the road trips and home games. As I got to know Kent I was shocked! He is trustworthy, a good listener, humble, lighthearted, and just an all-around pleasure to work with. How could a *sportswriter* have all these great qualities?

As a player you want a beat writer who will ask you something interesting, looking at different angles and ways to tell the story. You can only hope for a writer that has some character, one that won't lose the best interest of the player. You want someone you can trust with a little more information than the other writers because once you've been burned by someone you won't trust them again.

Kent was that guy. He made my years with the Bulls a pleasure. He was fair, tough when he needed to be, but even after a bad game I never worried about reading something unjustly negative or hurtful. And as we improved as a team, my relationship with Kent remained strong. We met at just the right moment.

In other words, our timing could not have been better.

—*Bill Cartwright*
May 2014

INTRODUCTION

In 1988, I was the midwest sports editor for United Press International in Chicago at the tender age of 32. Just 10 years out of college, I had the greatest job I could imagine, covering all Chicago sports, determining which games I worked and which ones I handed to stringers, writing columns and feature stories while overseeing sports coverage for eight Midwestern states.

But UPI was not a strong company financially, and I spent a great deal of my time dealing with stringers that were not getting paid, meanwhile worrying all the time about my own paycheck. There were consistent pay cuts and constant staffing problems and support issues. I was in charge of one deck on a sinking ship.

So when Tim Sassone, a colleague from the *Daily Herald* newspaper of Arlington Heights, Illinois, told me the paper was going major league with its sports coverage and suggested I apply for one of the available beat writer jobs, I was definitely interested. I had grown up reading the *Herald* and knew it was in position to compete with the two Chicago newspapers, the *Tribune* and *Sun-Times*. I was friendly with many of the employees who were covering the Chicago teams in their home games.

The *Herald* was known to me because I grew up in the northwest suburbs of Chicago, which eventually came to be known as "Herald City" by the people at the newspaper. When I was a kid, the *Herald* ran our school's lunch menu, and when I got into high school, I would occasionally get my name into the paper for running cross-country at Conant High School.

When I had my interview with sports editor Jim Cook at the *Herald*, I found out there were two jobs available, one covering the Chicago Bulls full time, and one covering college basketball and football. One job would have me traveling all over the country covering professional basketball, while the other would have me staying mostly in the Midwest covering Northwestern, Illinois, and Notre Dame in football, plus Illinois-Chicago, DePaul, and Loyola in college basketball.

I wanted the college job.

It was 1988, and I had already covered the Bulls for three years. I knew Michael Jordan superficially. I had a slight relationship with coach Doug Collins. I knew the NBA was growing in popularity, but I was like many others who did not know exactly what was going to become of the Bulls and Jordan.

Before moving to the Chicago area in 1967 at the age of 11, I grew up in Indianapolis and was a fan of Indiana University basketball. Indiana coach Bob Knight was like a god to me, and college basketball was the greatest of all games.

After graduating from DePauw University in Greencastle, Indiana, in 1978, I eventually became the Indiana state sports editor for UPI in Indianapolis before being transferred to Chicago, and during that time I covered the NBA's Indiana Pacers. My longstanding feeling about professional basketball was confirmed during those years: professional basketball is a bastardization of the great game I knew and loved. What the hell was "continuation"? How could referees call ticky-tack fouls on incidental contact and not call the muggings that went on under the basket on every single play?

On the other hand, covering college sports was the best. The spirit, the relative innocence, the feeling that every game mattered, it was impossible not to get caught up in the special feeling that college sports present. Football games are events, and even after covering games at Indiana, Purdue, and Notre Dame for five years, I still got completely psyched about covering a college football game.

College basketball, as I said before, was the sport of sports. Nothing would be better than covering Big Ten basketball. I could hardly wait.

Unfortunately, the *Herald* had another writer in mind for one of its two new positions and considered him a real "get." It was Bob Logan, the man who worked for the *Tribune* for a couple of decades and had been the first beat writer for the Bulls when they came into being in 1966. Surely, the *Herald* would reassign him to the Bulls, so that his expertise would be theirs to share with the Chicago suburban audience. The *Herald* would immediately have a name writer assigned to the beat for which he had already built a reputation.

But Logan was already in his fifties when the *Herald* hired him in 1988. Traveling with the Bulls was going to mean 41 games a year away from home, and usually those trips meant two days away from home. He had already been through that for years, and was not interested in that grind again.

I, on the other hand, was young and single (although I was dating my future wife and was two years away from marriage).

They offered me the Bulls job.

The pay raise, the opportunity to be on the inside as a full-time beat writer, and to travel the country with Jordan and the Bulls on someone else's dime, was something I could not turn down. So I said yes.

But I really wanted to cover college sports.

I'm going to say that it all worked out in the end.

1. First Days

I came into the job with the *Daily Herald* with a bit of a problem facing me.

Just a couple of weeks before I took the job, news broke that Jordan was a father. He had a baby boy with his girlfriend Juanita, but his public relations people had managed to keep it a secret from the public until a newspaper reporter finally broke the news. The reporter who broke the story was the man who covered the Bulls for the *Herald* the previous season, before they decided to travel with the team, before they hired me.

Somebody had told me that Jordan was pissed that his secret had been exposed. I assumed he was upset at the writer who broke the news, and I didn't want my new relationship to get off on the wrong foot because I was working for the same organization.

However, I also wanted to represent the *Herald* properly. The news was not incorrect. What Jordan had done was not illegal, but to his representatives, who guarded Jordan's reputation with vigor previously unseen in sports circles, it was not the kind of news they wanted public.

I am not one to let things linger. I would much rather get ugliness out of the way. It is my experience that things rarely turn out as bad as I think they are going to. And in this case, I was right.

Inside the Bulls locker room at Chicago Stadium before the first game I covered, I spoke to Jordan about the matter, and Jordan could not have been more pleasant. It helped that he knew me a little bit from the UPI job. Jordan might have harbored ill will toward the previous writer, but he had nothing to say to me on the issue. He may actually have been a bit relieved to have the news out there. Protecting a secret about a son born out of wedlock cannot be easy. It was soon thereafter that Michael married Juanita, and they went on to have two more children, Jeffrey and Jasmine, before their marriage dissolved in 2006.

Meanwhile, I had to ingratiate myself to everybody on the inside—the trainers, the equipment manager, the secretaries, and the assistant coaches. With UPI, I never really needed those people; my coverage was relatively basic. As a beat writer traveling with the team, I needed all the inside information I could get and as many sources as I could find.

Luckily, through my work with UPI, I already had a relationship with the public relations staff. That came in handy because those people really did know everything about everything, and sometimes they would tell me tidbits. They weren't going to let anything out that would get them fired, but sometimes the little stuff made good stories.

I felt the need to prove my credentials. I had spent those five years covering basketball in Indiana, and I had stories to tell about Bobby Knight (I was there when Knight threw a chair across the floor at Assembly Hall in Bloomington). I had covered the Pacers for those five years as well. I had covered basketball games at Hinkle Fieldhouse on the campus of Butler University. I had seen a lot of pro players when they were in high school or college.

It was a nervous time for me, but I was determined to prove I could handle the job. After all, it was writing about basketball. How hard could that be for a boy from Indiana?

With that Jordan controversy out of the way, I was ready to begin the greatest adventure of my life, covering the Chicago Bulls. I did not know that it would consume the next 11 years of my life.

Michael Jordan addresses the media after signing his rookie contract.

2. Bowling

When the Bulls started winning championships, things changed. The players became a bit more removed, partly for protection from fame scavengers and partly because I guess that is what incredibly famous people do.

But before they won their first championship in 1991, they were like every other team in the league. They had to beg for attention. They had to curry favor with fans. They had to be pleasant to sponsors.

In the 1980s, during the preseason, the Bulls would have a night out with the sponsors, and there was usually an activity involved. For a couple of years, it was bowling. The first year was 1988, and the Bulls rented out the Brunswick Lanes in Deerfield, adjacent to the practice facility where the Bulls trained. Every lane would have a sponsor, a broadcaster, and a media member, and the players and coaches would rotate through all the groups.

Because of their height, bowling is not a natural sport for the taller players. The guards, however, were all pretty good.

As you might guess, Michael Jordan did well. He picked up a 4-10 split on one lane, and on another he got a strike by throwing the ball through his legs from a running start. He said it was his first time bowling.

However, he was not the star of the night, at least according to my predecessor as the Bulls beat writer at the *Daily Herald*, Jim O'Donnell, who in 1988 was writing a media notes column for the paper:

"The unquestioned star of the night was new *Daily Herald* beat writer Kent McDill, who made six straight strikes and bowled a 207 to pace his squad to a convincing victory in the media-sponsors division."

In your face, Michael Jordan.

Our reward for victory was some bowling equipment and a bowling pin signed by all of the players on the team. Which is the only autograph I have of Michael Jordan—or Sam Vincent, for that matter.

Sam Vincent. The former Michigan State guard, played for the Bulls for two seasons from 1987 to 1989, but in 1988 he refused to bowl. He wasn't unpleasant about it. He did his time with the sponsors. But he had a perfectly good reason for refusing to play.

"Bowling is not a part of my cultural heritage," he said.

3. The Most Amazing Jordan Story of Them All

When point guard Randy Brown joined the Bulls in 1995 (on the same day they announced that Dennis Rodman joined, by the way), he came to the team after five seasons with the league-dragging Sacramento Kings. I knew him by reputation.

On my first chance to sit with him a couple of days after his introductory press conference, I had one question for Brown:

"Randy, I have been traveling with the Bulls since 1988, so I have been to Sacramento seven times, and I have never found anything to do there. So, what have you got for me?"

"I've got nothin'," Brown said with a laugh, and he went on to explain that Sacramento was the deadest town in the NBA, and that included Charlotte, which in the early 1990s when it joined the league still rolled up the sidewalks downtown at 9:00 PM.

But it turned out there was one thing you could do when you went to Sacramento, and that's go to Reno, Nevada, which is a two-hour drive away.

And so it was, during a lengthy seven-game road trip on the West Coast during the 1992–93 season, that former *Sun-Times* beat writer

Mike Mulligan and I planned to take a trip to Reno on the extra day we had in Sacramento.

The Bulls played the Utah Jazz on February 1 in Salt Lake City, and after the game, Mike and I talked to Michael Jordan in front of his locker at the Delta Center. The Bulls had won that night, so Jordan was in a good mood.

We asked Jordan what he was going to do in Sacramento for two days (the Bulls did not play the Kings until the night of February 3) and he rolled his eyes to indicate his disdain for visiting Sacramento.

"What are you guys going to do?" he asked.

"We're going to go to Reno tomorrow," Mulligan told him.

Jordan's eyes lit up. You have heard much over the years about Jordan's gambling habits, but you may never really understand just how much he enjoyed it. As a matter of fact, you are about to find out how much he enjoyed it.

"Here," he said, handing Mulligan a $100 bill. "Bet this for me on one hand of blackjack."

That was it. The end of the conversation.

So, on the next day, after writing our stories about the Bulls' practice from that afternoon, Mulligan and I took the two-hour drive from Sacramento to Reno. I remember a few things about the drive: I drove, and on the way Mulligan explained European soccer to me (little did I know six years later I would begin my true life's trek into soccer fandom).

But we talked a lot about the $100 bill. We had issues.

"What if we have to double down?"' Mulligan asked. That's where you get a 10 or 11 with your first two cards, the dealer is showing something under a seven, and you can double your bet. It's pretty much standard procedure. We decided in that situation we would have to cough up the $100.

"What if he gets aces or eights?" I asked. It is de rigueur to split a pair of aces or a pair of eights and play two hands against the dealer no matter what he is showing. Again, we realized we would have to come up with an extra $100.

Then we hit on the best idea we never actually put into place.

"What we should do is put the $100 down on 23 red [in roulette]," Mulligan said. "If we win, we get $3,500. We tell Michael he won his hand of blackjack, give him his $200 and split the rest."

This was a great idea, but it was also dishonest, and wrong. I told Mulligan so, and he begrudgingly agreed. That was more than 20 years ago, and Mulligan is still unhappy about the decision.

We got to Reno and entered Harrah's Casino. Since Jordan had given Mulligan the money, he was in charge of it.

Mulligan is a "feel" gambler and knew he was not going to play the $100 until he played a few hands at a blackjack table and felt he was playing against a giving dealer.

Before we played any blackjack, though, the first gaming table that appeared before us was a roulette table. I like roulette, and convinced Mulligan to sit and play a few rolls with me. We got our chips, spread them accordingly, and waited for the first spin.

Hand to God, it came up 23 Red.

I thought Mulligan was going to spontaneously combust. Then kill me.

Nobody at the table knew what we were laughing about, but we could not get over what had just happened.

We did not play Jordan's $100 for a long while. Mulligan played craps, and I played some video poker, and more blackjack. I actually had a killer run at the blackjack table that night, and at one point the dealer said to me, "Do you know you have won 13 hands in a row?" I knew I was going good, but that was big news for me. I'd never had a gambling moment like that before.

Finally, we decided it was time to find the table where we would gamble Jordan's money.

Mulligan and I each liked to sit at the end of the table, so I sat at the first spot of this one table and he sat at the last spot. We played a few hands, probably a dozen or so, and then Mulligan said my name.

"Here we go," he said. When we'd first arrived we had the $100 changed to a black chip to designate it as Jordan's money, and now Mulligan put that black chip down.

The cards were dealt. I looked at my first card, then looked over and saw that Mulligan had gotten a face card. My second card was turned, and I was trying to determine what my move was when Mulligan said, "Kent, look."

And there was beautiful King-Ace blackjack sitting in front of Mulligan.

He collected Jordan's $250, we played for a little while longer, and then went back to the Sacramento Hyatt.

Since Mulligan played the hand, it was agreed that he would get to tell Jordan what happened. And here is where the story gets a little spooky.

The morning of February 3, I was in the hotel lobby on my way to the workout room when I crossed paths with Jordan in the gift shop. He was getting ready to leave for the team's shootaround practice.

"Hey, Kent," he said. "What happened last night?"

I swear I was ready. I had promised Mulligan I would not tell him, and I didn't. But Jordan was very inquisitive.

"Did I win? Did I lose?" Jordan asked.

"I promised Mike I would let him tell you," I said.

And then Jordan came very close to me, bent down to put his face very close to mine, and looked me in the eyes. He then backed away slowly and said:

"I got blackjack."

I did not tell him, and Mulligan got the pleasure of handing over the $250 to Jordan, but the man knew. He knew.

4

108–101 Win Over Lakers Brings First NBA Title Home
June 13, 1991

INGLEWOOD, California—There is a first time for everything, and that's what the Bulls have won for the first time—everything.

The Chicago Bulls are NBA champions for the first time in their 25-year history. They shot the lights out of the Great Western Forum and shot down the theory that a team could not win the title on its first visit to the Finals.

The Bulls also crushed the rumor that they were a one-man team in their 108–101 win over the Los Angeles Lakers. Scottie Pippen outscored Michael Jordan 32–30 and guard John Paxson hit 5-of-6 jumpers in the fourth quarter to win the best-of-seven series 4–1.

"As an athlete you dream about something like this," said Paxson, who finished with 20 points. "It's unbelievable. The great thing is we did it as a team. We kept hearing we were a one-man team. But I think a championship will dispel that, at least until training camp."

"We've been trying to get rid of that stigma for a while," Jordan said. "Some of you guys said it was my fault for the way I play offense. But on national television, we won the championship as a team."

National television also showed a unique postgame celebration. The Bulls gathered in the visitor's locker room of the Great Western Forum and recited the Lord's Prayer, led by Bulls coach Phil Jackson. They then popped the corks on the champagne bottles.

"They were so poised all season long," Jackson said. "I think they just lost it."

Jordan won the Most Valuable Player trophy, which will match his MVP award for the regular season.

"I could care less about that," Jordan said. "It should go to the whole team."

The game came down to the fourth quarter, which started with an 80–80 tie. The last tie was at 93–93 and was broken, appropriately, by a Paxson 19-foot jumper with 3:54 remaining.

Sam Perkins, who had 12 points in the fourth quarter, missed a jumper from the free-throw line, and Paxson canned an 18-footer from the left corner to give the Bulls a 97–93 lead with 3:29 remaining.

Perkins missed a three-pointer with Paxson charging at him, and Paxson got the ball on an outlet pass for a layup and a 99–93 Bulls lead with 3:03 remaining.

The Lakers were within 103–101 with 1:13 left, but Paxson made an 18-footer with 56 seconds left. Perkins missed another three-pointer with 35 seconds left and the Bulls began celebrating.

Neither James Worthy nor Bryon Scott was in uniform as the game started. Lakers coach Mike Dunleavy had to go with A.C. Green, a former all-star, and Terry Teagle in the most important game of the season.

"For us to win the championship, all the starters had to play at the top of their capabilities as well as someone off the bench," Dunleavy said. "When this series came around, we came up a little flat."

The Lakers kept the lead for most of the first quarter, going ahead by 16–11 midway through the period. The Bulls fought back to a 23–23 tie on a jam by Jordan with 1:17 left in the period.

Dunleavy was quick to use the only two bench players he would use all night, Elden Campbell and Tony Smith. Campbell had 13 points in the first half while Smith hit three big baskets in the second quarter as the Lakers forged a 49–48 halftime lead.

Pippen made only 1-of-9 field goal tries in the first half but also came up with four steals.

The third quarter was more of the same, with the lead changing hands seven more times before Pippen scored on a driving layup with 8:02 left, giving the Bulls a 62–60 lead. After a Teagle miss, Pippen scored again on a runout, with an assist from Jordan, and the Bulls had a 64–60 lead.

The lead grew to 70–62 as Jordan made an 18-footer and Pippen stole the ball from Johnson and scored on a jam with 6:03 left. But the Lakers scored on a pair of three-pointers by Perkins and Magic Johnson to get back into the game.

5. Me and Michael Jordan

There is an oft-shown video clip from 1994 in which Michael Jordan is walking through the lower level corridors of the Chicago Stadium, being besieged by media wanting to get some sound from him.

Jordan was "retired" at the time. He was visiting the Barn to watch the Bulls play without him. He was training to be a baseball player, his future in basketball was only a dream, and he had been out of the public eye for some time.

In the video, you see Jordan walking briskly through the tunnel with cameramen and reporters following him. Jordan was not speaking to anyone, although he had a smile on his face. He was trying to get to a safe place where the cameras and reporters could not follow him.

He needed a distraction. That's when he saw me.

I was a reporter for the *Daily Herald* newspaper and had covered Jordan since 1988, traveling to every game the Bulls played. I had covered the three championships from 1991 to 1993. I knew Jordan and Jordan knew me.

I was not, however, trying to get a story out of Jordan. I was standing to the side, watching the media circus I usually tried to avoid. I knew if I needed something from him I could get it later when the crowd had dissipated.

But Jordan needed a distraction. So when he saw me standing off to the side to avoid the phalanx of media surrounding him, he walked over to me, with all the reporters and cameras following, and he put his arm around me and said hello. He then pushed me along with him as a way of having something to do besides avoid other people.

He was using me, clearly. The video shows that I don't particularly want to be in the video shots. But we walked together until he got to the locker room.

Orlando Woolridge congratulates Michael during his 63-point outburst against the Celtics in the Boston Garden. The 63 points set an all-time NBA playoff record for points scored in one game.

I had a relationship with all the members of the Bulls during the 11 years I traveled with them, and my relationship with Jordan was not my closest among the players. But I did provide some safety for Jordan, because I was not looking to trip him up or to dig beyond the stories that I needed. Jordan respected that, and often gave me some of his time when I asked, simply because I did not often ask.

There are many stories about me and Michael Jordan in this book. I was on the inside of the biggest story of the decade with the biggest athlete in the world as its centerpiece.

6. Scottie Pippen

I was working for UPI when Scottie Pippen and Horace Grant were selected in the first round of the NBA draft and brought to Chicago in the summer of 1987.

Eventually, they would both play a huge role in the success of the team and the championships that were on the way (three for Grant, six for Pippen). But it was Pippen that everyone came to see at the press conference.

Although he was selected fifth in the draft by the Seattle Super-Sonics and traded in a draft day deal with the Bulls, nobody outside of NBA experts really knew who Pippen was. He played his college ball at the University of Central Arkansas, an NAIA school that was not even a hotbed of basketball talent among NAIA schools. He had popped onto the radar of NBA scouts late in his college career.

Eventually, I would come to find out about Pippen's Arkansas upbringing in a tiny dirt-floor house with nine siblings and a wheel-chair-bound father. In an atmosphere where poor African American players were forced to adjust to an entirely new lifestyle with money and fame, Pippen came in as perhaps the poorest.

In the same way I couldn't forget how hard it was for Jerry Krause to be involved with the team because the players all hated him, I could never not consider Pippen's background when watching him as he adjusted to stardom and wealth.

What mattered from a basketball standpoint was Pippen's body. He was rail thin, but he was all limbs, long arms and long legs and long fingers. Krause, who on the day of Pippen and Grant's introduction in Chicago was enjoying perhaps his finest hour as general manager of the Bulls, could not stop talking about Pippen's length.

Pippen himself did not know who he was from an NBA standpoint when he came to the Bulls. His exposure to the league was in the pre-draft camp he attended in Portsmouth, Massachusetts, when he found out he could play with the big boys.

I'm sure there is some deep psychological reason for this, but I decided early on that I was going to work the Pippen connection. He wasn't even a starter when he got to the Bulls; coach Doug Collins was playing former Ohio State star Brad Sellers ahead of Pippen as a very skinny, very tall three (small forward), but I sensed Pippen was going to work his way into the lineup quickly. Teams do not ask No. 5 draft picks to sit on the bench for very long.

So I got to know him. As others were gathered around Jordan, whose locker was on the other side of the Chicago Stadium locker room from Pippen, I would make it a habit to ask Pippen questions after every game. I knew I would get Jordan's quotes; he was very good about standing and taking questions over and over until all of the reporters had exhausted themselves. But Pippen was going to be my go-to guy when I needed a voice other than Jordan's.

He recognized my effort. He was almost always pleased to see me. He answered my tough questions without rancor. I think he knew that

I was putting him in the same level of importance as Jordan in terms of covering the team.

In sportswriter parlance, when an athlete talks to a large group of reporters at his locker or coming off the practice floor, that is known as a gang-bang. It's an unfortunate part of what we do. While it is possible to get some usable quotes out of a gang-bang, the quotes you get are the same quotes everybody else in that gang-bang are getting.

As a beat writer, I was supposed to get stuff nobody else had. After a couple of years, I figured out that after the gang-bang, if I stood off to the side and waited, I could often get Jordan or Pippen to talk to me for an individual interview, if I didn't ask more than two or three questions. Besides, I'm a little weird about my questions. I try to go for just slightly off the wall remarks.

Pippen and Jordan also knew that they could trust me with the quotes. I was going to get them correct, and not try to turn them into something that was not truly said or meant.

It got to be a bit of a ritual with us. It made my job easier and helped me stand out a bit as I grew into the beat.

One day, after an unusually long gang-bang at the Berto Center, the Bulls practice facility, Pippen stepped away and saw me standing in my spot, waiting to ask a question that had not been touched in the throng interview.

"Why do you always do this?" he asked me smiling. "You are always here, waiting for me."

"I just want some alone time with you, Scottie," I said.

And he smiled. And we had our interview. And we had hundreds of them over the years.

7. MVP

A s this book is being written, the 2013–14 NBA season is underway. Kevin Durant of the Oklahoma City Thunder is making a big push to be considered as a candidate for Most Valuable Player, an award Miami Heat forward LeBron James has won four of the last five years.

The only blip on that list was in 2010–11, when Bulls guard Derrick Rose proclaimed himself an MVP candidate and then played the best season of his career. The media, which votes on the award and doesn't mind passing it around, chose Rose over James, although James had much the same season he'd had the previous two years and was just completing his first season as a member of the Miami Heat.

The media is not unwilling to vote for someone in order to not vote for someone else. That's what I was accused of in the 1996–97 season, when Michael Jordan lost out as MVP to Karl Malone of the Utah Jazz.

Jordan won his first MVP in 1988, before I was on the beat. He won his second in 1991 and again in 1992, when I voted for him. He did not win in 1993, when Charles Barkley personally carried the Phoenix Suns to the NBA Finals and to the brink of their first NBA championship before losing to Jordan and the Bulls.

Fast forward three years, and Jordan won again in 1996 after taking most of two seasons off to get his head together. That was his fourth NBA title.

In 1996–97, the Bulls and Utah Jazz were on a collision course to the NBA Finals, and the Jazz were led by Karl Malone, who averaged 27.4 points per game and shot 55 percent from the field.

Malone was an incredible player, and through his first 13 NBA seasons missed just five games. He was deserving of admiration, but did he deserve an MVP award?

Apparently, he did, because Malone won the award that year, with Jordan finishing second. Jordan averaged 29.6 points that season, the first time since his third year in the league he did not average at least 30 points per game when playing an entire season. He shot 48.6 percent from the field, one of his lowest percentages in his career.

The Bulls had a better record than Utah, 69 wins to 64 wins, but Jordan had another Hall of Famer with him in Scottie Pippen. Then again, so did Malone, with John Stockton as his running mate. But the Bulls and Jordan had Dennis Rodman, and the Jazz, well, they didn't have Dennis Rodman.

So I made my pick, I wrote a column about it for the newspaper, and I let it go. I could justify the pick, and I really believed that Utah without Malone would be much worse than the Bulls without Jordan. I would gladly talk about the pick on sports radio, which I did.

What happened next was unexpected. Malone won, and Chicago exploded.

The idea that anyone other than Jordan could win the MVP award, especially after he made such a triumphant comeback in 1995–96 to lead the Bulls to title No. 4, was ludicrous. Who voted for Malone, the fan base asked?

One week after our votes were in and two weeks before the award was announced, the Salt Lake City afternoon newspaper the *Deseret News* polled all of the voters and got all of them to say publicly who they voted for. They announced before the NBA did that Malone was going to be the winner.

The *Deseret News* went one step further. When they pre-announced the winner, they told the world that the three Chicago-area voters—myself, Terry Armour of the *Chicago Tribune*, and John Jackson of the *Chicago Sun-Times*—all voted for Malone. That was world news.

We were traitors. We were biased against Jordan (for some reason). We were voting for Malone in order to get attention.

That was not the case, at least in my decision, although I did get a lot of attention. I know Armour tried to keep his pick secret, while Jackson did write about it in a column after the award was announced and the news broke.

The day after the news, I did a segment on the Chicago sports radio station The Score, which asked if I would be willing to take calls. I did. It did not help my feeling of self-worth.

Bulls coach Phil Jackson publicly decried the vote, although he kept my name out of it.

"We won 69 games this year mostly on the energy of Michael and Scottie [Pippen]," Jackson said. "We had mishaps with Dennis [Rodman] and Luc Longley, so we were not together as a unit the whole year. Karl played with that unit the whole season, and they had no injuries. He did his job, there's no doubt about it, but for the excess weight that was put on our team and still to win 69 games, there's no earthly explanation except that Michael won it so many times and this may be Malone's opportunity."

And Jordan's reaction?

He had a day to absorb it before he spoke publicly, but he shook my hand when he saw me and tossed my hair, which he always used to do. Then, when asked about the vote, he said, "I would have voted for Karl, too."

In 1991, when Jordan was under consideration for his second MVP award (which had gone to Magic Johnson the two years previous), he admitted the entire process seemed weird to him.

"I don't know how you guys [the media] vote," he told me. "I'll just play the game and let you guys vote."

"Whoever helps a good basketball team get in position for a world championship," he said. "How much the player means to the team. If he was not with the team, where would that team be? That's my most valuable player."

8. The Multiplex

When I first started covering the Bulls, it was at a time when teams were still flying commercial, and teams trained where they could find space. It wasn't until the early 1990s that teams started building their own facilities for private workouts.

From 1985 to 1992, the Bulls trained in a private health club in the north suburb of Deerfield named the Multiplex. Every space the Bulls used for training—the gymnasium, the workout room, the pool—was used by health club members when the Bulls were done with it for the day. In 1990, they built their own facility just half a mile from the Multiplex, which became known as the Berto Center, named after Sheri Berto, a longtime assistant to team owner Jerry Reinsdorf.

In 2013, the Bulls announced plans to move their practice facility downtown, just east of the United Center, to accommodate the players, most of whom lived in downtown Chicago.

When the Bulls practiced at the Multiplex, they used the first-floor space on the north end of the club, which was situated inside a shopping mall. There was no security, although there was an unwritten rule among members not to gawk or gather around the team as it practiced.

The media had a small room off the gymnasium that they were allowed to use as a press room, but it was a converted closet for equipment. There were no press conferences in that room; it was barely big enough for a conversation.

The gymnasium was enclosed in glass, but the practices were right there for all to see if they chose to do so. The reporters who would gather got to know when something might be taking place that they actually needed to see, but unless there were shoving matches or an injury occurred, watching practice was not much fun.

There were tennis courts at the Multiplex, and I used to play the game. I liked to think I was good enough that I didn't mind putting myself out there to challenge anyone who might come along.

As it turned out, Craig Hodges came along. The long-range shooter who played for the Bulls from 1988 to 1992 was an excellent all-around athlete and a decent tennis player. I'm pretty sure I beat him when we played, but he may remember it differently. Later, the Bulls signed another long-range shooter, Trent Tucker, and I played with him on several occasions. Trent beat me, though. Of that I'm sure.

Many times, injured players were encouraged to use the swimming pool to stay in shape. Minor leg injuries were often treated that way. They didn't do much swimming; it was more just walking around.

Many of the African American players were vocal about not liking swimming, and a number of them didn't know how. Among those who couldn't swim?

Michael Jordan.

In a 1992 interview with *Playboy* magazine conducted by my colleague Mark Vancil, Jordan said he was swimming with a friend in the ocean when the friend went under a current and died. It was at that point Jordan decided he was never going to go in the water again.

Jordan did not go into the water, did not take the trainers' advice to swim in order to repair minor aches and pains. He would sit in the pool area and kibitz with his teammates, even mocking those who tried to swim. But he wasn't going to join them.

9. What Scares Michael Jordan

Certainly, when Jordan was playing, he was considered a Superman to so many of his fans. His basketball skills were beyond compare, and his will to win was his strongest attribute.

But, as noted, he had his fears, and swimming was one of them. But he also had a fear of illnesses, and hated hearing about new ones.

For many years, Lacy J. Banks covered the Bulls for the *Chicago Sun-Times*. He was an old-school newspaper man, and had covered the Bulls from before I was on the beat. He was older than me, and not the healthiest man in the world. He was famous for ordering room service at our hotel on road trips so that he could have a meal waiting for him when he got back. Eating a full meal at 11:00 PM is never recommended.

Banks had a history of kidney stones, and had an attack while covering the Bulls. He missed several games while in recovery but made his return one day when the Bulls were playing the Hawks in Atlanta. When reporters were allowed into the locker room pregame, Jordan asked Banks where he had been.

"I was in the hospital," Banks said.

"What for?" Jordan asked.

"I had to pass a kidney stone," Banks said.

Jordan asked Banks what a kidney stone was, and Banks told him that it was a hardened mass of phosphates that get to be the size of a green pea.

"So what do you do?" Jordan asked. "Do you [poop] it out?"

Banks laughed. "No, it passes through your penis. And it hurts."

And at this point, Jordan instinctively crossed his legs.

"I don't want to get kidney stones. How can I avoid getting them?"

"Well, I have been told that fresh fruit helps."

"Somebody get me a banana, quick!" Jordan exclaimed. And he was serious.

We all have fears, and Jordan has one of the more popular ones, the fear of snakes.

Jordan's son Marcus tells the story of how he and his older brother Jeffrey would get plastic snakes and place them around the house to shake up the old man.

Bulls equipment manager John Ligmanowski was perhaps the least known significant player in the history of the championship Bulls. "Ligs" had a special relationship with Jordan, and it included the fact that he always kept a very lifelike rubber snake in his equipment bag that he could place in Jordan's locker whenever he felt in the mood.

10. Traveling

In 2014, professional athletes in the major sports leagues have it good from a traveling aspect.

They fly in charter planes that use set-off terminals. While they can be victimized by weather, they can't be delayed because another flight from New Orleans has not yet come in. They stay in top-flight hotels and are waited on hand and foot by hotel personnel, airport personnel, and stadium personnel.

But those types of amenities for NBA players did not come into vogue until the early 1990s. I had several years covering the Bulls where their travel plans and disappointments almost always dovetailed with my own.

In the modern NBA, teams fly to their destination city the night before a game, stay in a fancy hotel, play their game, then fly home the night of the game. The teams are mandated by the league to be in the host city the night before the game so that any flight difficulties due to weather can be avoided.

In 1988, teams did not fly on charter flights. They flew on commercial flights, and since there were no commercial flights available at 11:00 PM or midnight after a game, they were forced to spend the night in the town in which they played. Therefore, to avoid a two-night hotel stay, they would fly into town the morning of a game, hoping the weather and the foibles of commercial flights would not stymie them.

So, if a private citizen was on a morning flight from, say, Cleveland to Chicago, they could be on the same flight as the Cavaliers going to the Windy City or the Bulls returning home after a game in Ohio.

There were no special accommodations for teams flying on commercial flights, either. They waited for the plane in the same non-descript waiting area as regular passengers, they boarded in the same way, and they often crammed themselves into the same seats as a regular passenger.

NBA teams in 1988 had at least 12 players, three or four coaches, an athletic trainer and an equipment manager flying together. Coaches were given the first available first class seats, then veteran players, and status was determined not by points per game but by seasons played. In 1988, Jordan was in his fourth season in the NBA, and in 1988 there were many players on the team who had more years of service than Jordan did.

So, on that aforementioned flight from Cleveland to Chicago, you could have had an economy seat and sat next to Michael Jordan. Flights from Cleveland to Chicago, or Chicago to Detroit, or Indianapolis, usually had no more than eight first-class seats, and often those seats were taken by regular customers.

Like the old lady who sat next to Bill Cartwright, the seven-foot center acquired by the Bulls in 1988 to give them the post presence they did not have. The flight was from one Western Conference location to another (I know we ended up in San Antonio) and had few first class seats. But Cartwright, a 10-year veteran when he joined the Bulls, had one of them. In fact, his assigned seat was an aisle seat, which he needed to have extra room for his long legs.

Because I spent a lot of time with Cartwright while he was with the Bulls, he and I entered the plane at the same time, and I was behind him as he prepared to get into his seat. The little old lady was already in her window seat, and she was agitated, not by Cartwright's appearance, but by her seat selection.

"Would you mind trading seats with me?" she asked Cartwright before he could sit down. "Sitting by the window gives me the heebie-jeebies."

Cartwright agreed to do so, and squeezed himself into the first class window seat after the woman got up. Luckily, it was a short flight.

At the end of flights, the team would gather at luggage claim and wait for their bags to roll to them on the carousel. Michael Jordan, with a known penchant for gambling, would make a wager with teammates regarding whose bag would come off first. Michael usually won.

But Michael also usually cheated, especially when the Bulls were traveling from Chicago to elsewhere. He made arrangements with luggage personnel at O'Hare Airport to make sure his bag was the first team bag off the flight upon its arrival in the destination city. Packed last on departure, it was unpacked first upon arrival, and Jordan would win his money from unsuspecting teammates.

The flights themselves could sometimes get rowdy, especially if Jordan and teammates were in the back of the plane. Jordan would arrange games of Tonk, a card game that would include a gambling component. The game required cards be thrown down in a discard pile, and when teammates were on opposite sides of the aisle, the discard pile

29

was in the aisle. Flight attendants had to coordinate their time for going to the back of the plane so as not to disturb the game.

Once the team arrived in an NBA city, there was usually a bus waiting to transport the team to the hotel. The team would make a quick stop to their rooms, then prepare for a shootaround practice or, if we arrived too late for that, to get to the stadium in time for some pregame work.

But as anyone with a travel history knows, travel plans don't always follow the scheduled path. Such was the case when the Bulls had a game in Charlotte on January 11, 1989.

We had played the Atlanta Hawks in Atlanta the night before, and were at Hartsfield Airport preparing for our early morning flight to Charlotte. For some geographic reason, Charlotte suffers from regular attacks of fog. It was by far one of the more difficult NBA stops to get to because of weather, even more so than the cold-weather stops.

Flights were backed up, and no one knew for sure whether we would get into Charlotte on time for the game. So the Bulls hired a bus to drive the team to Charlotte, a four-hour trip by bus. They were kind enough to let me join them.

We embarked on a four-hour trek by bus from Atlanta to Charlotte. As you might guess, the players were completely juvenile about the entire thing, yelling like school kids going on a field trip.

There was a lot of discussion about who was going to sit where: this was different than a hotel-to-airport ride, and the guys in the back had serious card-playing plans.

We were not going to get into Charlotte until well after noon, and coach Doug Collins wanted the team to be fed when we arrived in town. This being 1989, and no Internet available to search for available restaurant options, we did what all interstate travelers did in those days: we stopped at McDonald's.

(Actually, any other team might have stopped at the Wendy's that we drove by, or the Burger King that was closer to the highway. But Jordan saw a McDonald's sign on the road, and since he had an endorsement contract with McDonald's, he declared that McDonald's was where we were going to stop.)

The bus had no identifiers on it, so the people inside had no idea the Chicago Bulls were pulling up, or that Michael Jordan was on the bus. In fact, they never found out Jordan was on the bus.

As we exited, we were instructed by the trainer, Mark Pfeil, not to mention that Jordan was with us. We were to say he had taken a special car to get to Charlotte.

But Jordan wanted to eat. So he gave rookie Jack Haley his order, and then slinked down into the seat to prevent any onlookers from catching a view of him.

I worked at McDonald's as a high schooler, and I remember how we responded when a large group of people came in. It was all hands on deck, produce as much food as possible as quickly as possible. But I can't imagine what management thought when they saw guys like Cartwright (7'1"), Will Perdue (7'), and Dave Corzine (6'11") walk into the place.

We ate on the bus, which made the rest of the trip odor-ific. But we got to Charlotte in time for the Bulls to beat the Hornets.

11. Jerry Krause

They called him "Crumbs" as a way to suggest he always had crumbs on his clothing because of his eating habits. It was a way to put him down.

His real name was Jerry Krause, and he was the general manager of the Chicago Bulls from 1985 to 2003. He was apparently good at his

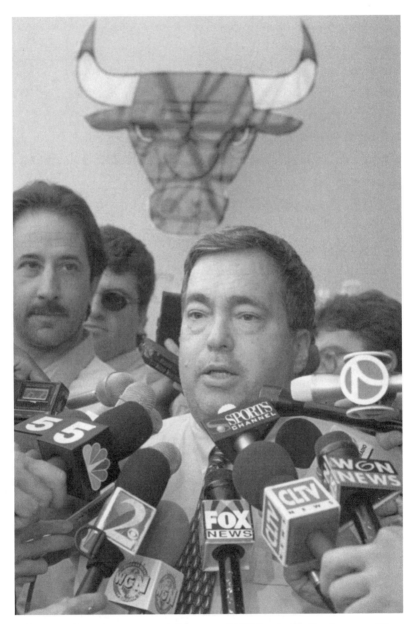

Jerry Krause discusses the trade that sent Will Purdue to the Spurs, netting the Bulls Dennis Rodman.

job. He was the man who put together the rosters that eventually won six NBA titles. He not only created one championship roster for the team that won the titles in 1991, '92, and '93, he created another championship roster that won the titles from 1996 to '98.

No, he did not play basketball. And no, he was not the only person responsible for the Bulls winning championships. He never even suggested he was the only person responsible for the Bulls winning championships. People like to say he did, but they're wrong.

In a world of tall men, Krause stood out because he was not tall. He was squattish (whenever we played the "Who would play what role when this long, strange trip becomes a movie" game, Danny DeVito was always chosen to play Krause), and perhaps he did not need to do much squatting when he played catcher on baseball teams in high school and college, because he did not have far to squat. He was in no way personable; he was secretive and guarded, suspicious, gruff, and prideful.

Krause had no real use for the media, but his job required him to have dealings with us. So he did. No one in the media ever got anything useful out of him.

While he never gave out useful information to the media, he was especially terse in regards to questions about player acquisition. There were two reasons for that:

- Player identification was his bailiwick, his ball game. His status and regard in the National Basketball Association was totally determined by his ability to identify talent good enough to make it and thrive in the world of professional basketball. He loved finding the player no one else had on their radar.
- Krause knew that no good could come from confirming or denying media reports about player acquisition plans. Confirming

an interest in a player would negatively affect negotiations, taking away some of his advantage; denying an interest in a player would hamstring him in future conversations, because any player he would NOT deny interest in would be a player he apparently DID have interest in.

Krause would never say anything about his interest in players, either in college or in the pros, so that he was never put in a position of getting caught in a lie. Silence is a powerful tool in negotiations and is value-neutral.

"Here's the thing," Krause told me. "If you come to me with a trade rumor and I deny it because it is not true, and then later you come to me with a trade rumor that has substance and I don't say anything, I am confirming the rumor by not denying it. Or I am required to lie to you. It's best for me not to say anything."

And so he didn't.

While he had working relationships with many people in the Bulls front office, and there were people who accepted him and understood him, he received very little love among the players. In most cases, he received disregard or outright verbal abuse. It was almost as if he was being bullied, despite his position of power and influence.

From the first three-peat roster, veteran center Bill Cartwright was the closest thing Krause had to an amiable relationship, because Cartwright was mature enough to accept Krause for his manner and because Krause saw value in him and proclaimed him to be the missing piece of the puzzle to lead the Bulls to a title when he traded Charles Oakley to get him from the New York Knicks in the summer of 1988.

From the second three-peat roster, only Toni Kukoc noticeably gave Krause the time of day. Krause was responsible for bringing Kukoc over from Europe. While Kukoc was a very good basketball player, Krause made him seem great, promoting him as his next great find, which irritated Jordan and Pippen, and put Kukoc in a bad position from a team standpoint. Jordan and Pippen were loath to appreciate any player that Krause pitched, and because Krause's pitch about Kukoc was so complimentary and promotional, Kukoc was seen as an interloper of sorts. Eventually, Kukoc's extremely pleasant personality and his ability to play won everybody over. But Kukoc would visibly wince whenever he heard someone mock Krause.

I'm not certain if Krause had warm relations with any member of the media (he used to give Bob Ryan from Boston kudos all the time for being a stand-up guy) but my relationship with him was positive. I came to realize the topics upon which he might actually give me something useful, the topics upon which he would not participate, and otherwise kept my distance.

I also could not help but feel bad for him because he was stuck in a very visible situation with a lot of people who did not like him and weren't afraid to let it be known. The players openly mocked him, and fans never warmed to him, even when the Bulls started winning titles. I knew him to be a man who wanted to do his job well and just wanted to be recognized for it, and neither of those desires seemed to me to be a sin.

Krause's unwillingness to offer the media much of anything in the way of information served him well, but it was the media that proved to be his final undoing. Krause cemented his place in Chicago when, during the first three-peat, he was quoted as saying, "Players don't win championships alone; organizations win championships." It was not only a true statement (as you think about the long list of great players who never won titles) it is also a fairly tame remark. It's kind of obvious. You need front-office personnel to make the deals and acquire the players who then win the games on the court.

However, somewhere very quickly after he made the statement, Krause was ripped to shreds among some media and a great percentage of fans for trying to erase the significance of the players' accomplishments. That's not what he did, but if you take the word "alone" out of his quote, as some people did, suddenly it appears as if Krause was trying to declare that the organization "alone" won the titles, and since he was the leader of the organization, he was the de facto reason the Bulls won titles.

All Krause wanted was a little acknowledgement that he played a significant role in the success of the team. He was never going to get it; only his best friend and benefactor, Bulls owner Jerry Reinsdorf, would ever give Krause sincere public acknowledgement of his achievements, and did so by putting a banner in the rafters of the United Center with his name on it.

In his prideful Hall of Fame speech, Jordan made it clear what he thought of Krause.

"Jerry Krause is right there. I don't know who invited him. I didn't. I hope he understands it goes a long way, and he was a very competitive person and I was a very competitive person. He said 'organizations win championships.' I said, 'I didn't see organizations playing with the flu in Utah. I didn't see them playing with a bad ankle.' Granted, I think organizations put together teams, but at the end of the day, the team has to go out and play."

In a public relations battle between Michael Jordan and Jerry Krause, who do you think would win? It was never going to be Krause.

All of this background, all of the years I spent watching Krause and working with him, and all of my feelings about how difficult Krause's life was as general manager of the Bulls, came to mind the one time Krause and I had lunch together.

It was during the second three-peat. Krause had already seen success and was enjoying the remarkable accolades that came from rebuilding the championship team around Jordan and Pippen and managing to create yet another roster of talented players who could and would set aside personal statistics in order to win championships. He had found Ron Harper, Steve Kerr, Randy Brown, and Bill Wennington; he had drafted Toni Kukoc; he had agreed to bring hated Detroit Piston Dennis Rodman to town. At that time, everything he did worked, and he still struggled to get credit from anyone for what he had done.

So after practice one day we went to a nice Jewish deli just a few blocks from the Bulls' practice facility in Deerfield, Illinois. It was a pleasant meal, we had a pleasant conversation, and showed just how successful our relationship of complete non-disclosure was.

But, as he picked up his large deli sandwich for the first bite, some ingredients fell out—a piece of lettuce with mayonnaise or mustard on it. It fell into his lap. I pretended not to notice.

And then, under his breath, Krause revealed some of the personal struggle he battled daily. He looked into his lap, grabbed at his napkin, and whispered "Will you look at that?"

He was Crumbs, one of the best, hardest-working, and least appreciated general managers in the history of the NBA.

12. The First Championship Locker Room

There are beat writers who work for 30 years and never get to cover a championship team. I'm thinking about guys who cover the NBA in places like Cleveland or Sacramento. They toil just as I did, but see very few meaningful games. It's their job to make the games seem important, and when an NBA season drags on, that is definitely a chore.

During my 11 years with the Bulls, every year had a significant theme. The first three years were watching the Bulls grow as Jordan and Pippen and Grant and Cartwright learned to play with each other. They had to figure out how to get past the Detroit Pistons in the Eastern Conference, which they finally did in 1991, after losing to the Pistons in both the 1989 and 1990 conference playoffs.

The title seasons were easy covers from the standpoint of stories to tell. We did not know the significance of the first until it happened, but every step of the journey to the first title was memorable. The second one was to prove they could repeat, which is the mark of a truly talented team and validates the first title. The third title creates a dynasty, and that story was a long one, as most of the team dealt with injuries along the way.

After three title seasons, there were two seasons without Jordan following his first retirement. The first one was a focus on Pippen, to see if he could lead a team to a championship, which he might have done if not for an unusually called game in New York in the Eastern Conference Semifinals in the spring of 1994.

The next season, after Jordan had played a summer of baseball, there was all the talk that he was coming back to the Bulls. By this time, Bulls general manager Jerry Krause had completed the rebuild of the team, creating a roster that would eventually be the team around which Jordan and Pippen were able to win three more titles.

Then Jordan came back and the end of that season was interesting because Jordan was not ready to play, not like he was before. The Bulls lost to Orlando in the 1995 Eastern Conference Semifinals, and Jordan rededicated himself to be ready for the following season.

So the Bulls acquired Dennis Rodman in the summer of 1995 and there were three more seasons of championships. I got to witness all of that history.

Michael holds the Larry O'Brien Trophy aloft, talking to reporters after the Bulls victory over the Lakers in the 1991 NBA Finals.

Which means I got to enter six championship locker rooms.

The first one was in Los Angeles, where the Bulls completed a five-game NBA Finals win over the Lakers. This was at the Great Western Forum, which was a stadium marvel when it was built but was on its last legs by 1991. The visiting locker room was small, but that is where Jordan and the Bulls celebrated their first title.

I was there when Jordan lay on the floor of the locker room crying. I was there when he hugged the Lawrence O'Brien Trophy. I was covered in champagne for the first time in my life.

It was exciting, but keep in mind, I was working, and I was covering my first title of any sort. I was trying to get unique quotes from players who were enjoying the biggest moment of their lives from an athletic standpoint. I was thinking about storylines. I was not drinking champagne; I was trying to keep it out of my eyes and off my notebook and tape recorder.

I had to talk to all five starters: Jordan, Scottie Pippen, Horace Grant, John Paxson, and Bill Cartwright. It was a whirl, but there was one moment I will always remember.

Bill Cartwright and I had an interesting relationship; at the time, I would count him as the second-best relationship I had with a player. We sat with each other on the team bus, me in the last row of the media seats and Cartwright in the first seats for players. Our talks on the bus were always interesting. He liked to argue, not because he was mean-spirited, just because he enjoyed the banter that comes from a good disagreement.

But not on June 12, 1991. Cartwright was playing in his 12th NBA season and had just won his first title. He would eventually be credited as one of the missing pieces the Bulls had to have to be a successful team. He would never be one of the guys, but he was one of the champions.

I approached him to get his reaction to the victory. I knew it was going to be difficult to get a quote from him; his gravelly voice would be hard to hear in the bedlam that was surrounding us. He could not speak with volume. He also tended to be thoughtful in his comments and you often had to wait for him to gather his thoughts.

Cartwright was very alone on the Bulls. He was older than almost everybody, and he was more mature as well. He wasn't a part of the team's tomfoolery. He was the target of jokes (Stacey King made fun of his voice on almost every bus trip). He did not have anyone to celebrate with.

Then he saw me. And the emotion of all of those years in the league, and all the abuse he took as Patrick Ewing's backup in New York and as the guy that made Charles Oakley leave the Bulls swelled upon him.

As I approached him, he grabbed me around the shoulders. For some reason, he turned me around, then hugged me from behind. He hugged me for several seconds. It was the most demonstrative thing I ever saw him do. That he did it to me made me understand just how alone he was on the team. But I guess I served a purpose.

The rest of that night will live in infamy. The team was staying at a Marina Del Rey Hotel, which had balconies, and apparently there were some shenanigans up there, as players decided the balconies were the best way to go from room to room, as opposed to the more conventional hallway. The party reportedly did not end until after the team flew home to Chicago the next day.

A couple of days later, the Bulls started an unusual tradition of having a celebration in Grant Park rather than having a ticker-tape parade. The first one I attended, I managed to get backstage and shook some players' hands, then had to go back into the crowd to hear what the players were saying to the gathered masses.

Chicago police estimated the crowd at 1 million people. I don't know if they counted correctly, but it was the first title celebration in Chicago since the 1985 Chicago Bears, and the city wanted to make sure the Bulls knew how much they were appreciated.

13. Famous Reporters

There was a modicum of fame that came with covering the most famous athlete in the world and the best professional sports team of its time.

Because I had an insiders' point of view, I did countless TV and radio shows, and sometimes even got paid for doing them. I appeared on radio shows in NBA cities around the country, finally getting a chance to use the Broadcast Communications degree I got from DePauw University.

In the northwest suburbs of Chicago, where the *Daily Herald* was distributed and trusted and well-read, I was a little itty-bit of a star. The *Daily Herald* had a speaker's bureau at the time, and I was often requested to regale large groups of people with the kinds of stories I am telling you here, only I saved the best for the readers of this book. Don't let those people know I was holding back.

My picture ran with my weekly NBA column, and I was on TV once in a while, but it still amused me to be recognized in public.

One night, my wife and I went to see a movie. The ticket taker was a young man, I'm guessing college age, and when he saw me his face lit up.

"Are you Kent McDill?" he said, asking me the one question to which I always answer "Yes," which I did.

"I read you every day. You're a really good writer," he said.

I thanked him, and as we walked past I turned to my wife and said, "If I was single and on a date, I'd be getting lucky tonight."

My wife just said, "Let's go see the movie" and that was the end of that episode.

Sometime during the first three-peat, we were in Denver, and Tribune reporter Melissa Isaacson and I were getting ready to get a cab to take us to the Pepsi Center for the game. We got down to the bell stand and the bellhop said, "It will take a while to get a cab [some cities are like that], but we do have a stretch town car available. Would you like that?" We asked about cost, which was similar to a taxi, so we took it, arriving at the game in style.

Our driver's name was Tony, and he told us he could pick us up after the game if we gave him 10 minutes' notice. So as Isaacson and I were wrapping up our computers and getting ready to leave after the game, I called Tony and told him to meet us where he dropped us outside the arena.

As we waited outside of the Pepsi Center, a member of the Nuggets' media relations staff came walking by and asked us if we needed a ride. We declined, saying we had a ride coming, and then he asked us conversationally if there were any perks for reporters who cover such a famous team. It was at that exact moment that Tony drove up in the very luxurious vehicle. As Tony opened the door for us, I turned to him and said, "Yes, there is."

Isaacson and I laughed all the way back to the hotel.

I do have to say that I found my modicum of fame amusing and in some cases just plain wrong. There are media members who become superstars in their own right, and perhaps I have a bit of jealousy toward them because I never became internationally acclaimed, but all sportswriters do is detail the athletic accomplishments of others. We tell stories, and we don't even make them up. We provide information for people who are not on the inside. But we don't do anything extraordinary.

That being said, I would have gladly accepted my own radio show.

14. Vegas

There was a time when the National Basketball Association was considering putting a team in the gambling capital of the United States: Las Vegas, Nevada. The country is running out of communities that meet the necessary standards of population, average net worth, and physical space to support the financial needs of major sports franchises, and Vegas seemed like a logical choice, if you could get past the difficulty that gambling might cause.

No team is in Vegas yet, but the NBA courts the Vegas crowd by hosting a summer league in the city every year, and when I was traveling with the Bulls, we twice played preseason games in the city that truly never sleeps (because of the oxygen they pump into our systems). The first time I traveled with the Bulls to Las Vegas was with the first three-peat team, and it was relatively sedate. A good time was had by all, to be sure, but I don't recall any real stories of players misbehaving. I do know Phil Jackson altered his practice schedule to accommodate the after-hours needs of players, but Jackson was always the thinking man's coach.

The second time we went to Vegas, Dennis Rodman was on the team, and if Rodman and Jordan had anything in common, it was their ability to enjoy Las Vegas. Jordan enjoyed it for the gambling aspect, while Rodman enjoyed it for the big lights and night life and the gambling.

Rarely in my years of covering the Bulls had I seen a bunch of players get dressed quicker than they did after the meaningless preseason game in Las Vegas. Apparently, they had plans for the evening postgame. Reporters, too, made quick work of their interviews and stories. It was a preseason game, after all, and there were more important games to be played back on The Strip.

Somehow, I spent much of the evening alone. I don't do much in the way of gambling other than cheap blackjack and video poker. I am more of a bright lights guy, digging on the scene along The Strip.

But I did run into Rodman twice that night, first at the start, and then at the very end.

After I washed up in my hotel room following the game, I went down to the casino at the Mirage Hotel where we were staying. The first thing I saw was Rodman standing at the top point of a craps table, and somehow he managed to see me walk into the room. He called me over to help him win some cash.

Which I apparently did. I don't play craps; despite having a fairly decent understanding of all things having to do with numbers, I just don't get it. But Rodman had me handle the dice for a while, and it went well enough that he pounded me on the back a few times, pleased with my performance. I had absolutely no idea what I was doing, and I wasn't gambling. I was just aiding and abetting, I guess.

Then I turned cold, the dice were taken away from me, and I stood there for a few more minutes, up until the point I was attacked.

From somewhere behind me, a pair of hairless arms wrapped around my midsection, and I was suddenly and abruptly lifted off the ground. I was swung around so that I was facing away from the craps table.

I turned back to see what had just happened, and saw a very attractive tallish woman standing where I had been standing next to Rodman. I recognized her arms; she had been the one to lift me out of my spot. She looked at me with a glance that would have needed significant improvement to be considered disdainful.

Rodman looked at me. Then he looked at her. Then he looked at me. He smiled, shrugged, and went on with what he was doing. My night at the craps table with Dennis Rodman was over. I had been replaced.

Several hours later, I was trying to finish with a positive experience and playing video poker in a very quiet part of the Mirage casino. I was virtually alone, but not ready to call it a night.

I heard a disturbance behind me and looked down the wide aisle between the video poker and slot machines and saw two tightly wrapped women walking in front of two tall men. The men were Rodman and his personal bodyguard, whose name was George.

What they were doing with the women was this: the women would stop in front of Rodman and George, and bend slightly at the waist to point their backseats toward the men. The men would then slap the women on the butt, and the women would prance merrily a few steps away with high giggles before setting up again for another slap.

It was almost like a processional.

Rodman did not see me see him. They went past me without a word, and I was reminded of a line from the movie *Diner*, when Kevin Bacon and Mickey Rourke were talking to the very rich young woman on horseback, and as she rode away, Bacon said, "Do you ever get the feeling there's something going on we don't know about?"

Perhaps I was being reminded just why the NBA and other professional sports leagues do not have permanent teams calling Las Vegas home.

15. Drinking With Jordan

Sportswriters have an image problem. Perhaps it dates to the portrayal of Oscar in The *Odd Couple*. We are supposed to be slovenly, rotund, uncouth and focused only on sports.

Oh, and we drink a lot of beer.

Over the years, I did indeed enjoy nights out on the road that included consuming alcohol. I almost never did so with athletes. They had their own places to go, and they did not mind not having us around. They wanted to let their hair down, and even when they trusted us, they knew we might be tempted to tell stories about what we saw.

My personal rule, however, was that anything that happened that did not require a police report would stay unpublished. At least until this book, I guess.

But, also, there was stuff I did not want to know. If married players were messing around with women to whom they were not married, I really, really did not want to know that. While extra-marital liaisons are morally wrong, they are not against the law. So I stayed away from situations that would allow me to find out that kind of information.

On only two occasions that I can recall did I have a drink with Michael Jordan. It wasn't like we avoided each other; Jordan just didn't go out much and when he did it was rarely at the same place I was. But I was available. All he had to do was call.

The first time we had a beer together was a night that would forever live in the annals of Jordan's greatest nights. It was March 28, 1990, in Cleveland, when Jordan made 23-of-37 shots and finished with his career high 69 points in a 117–113 overtime victory over the Cavaliers. It currently ranks 11th on the list of individual scoring performances in a regular season game, and six of the games ahead of Jordan's 69 were performed by Wilt Chamberlain, who averaged 50 points per game in one season. The others were turned in by Kobe Bryant, David Thompson, Elgin Baylor, and David Robinson. Jordan still holds the record for most points in a playoff game with 63, a game the Bulls lost against the Boston Celtics.

On nights when Jordan did something amazing, I had to turn up my own performance as a sportswriter. It was not enough to write a simple story about what happened; I had to trumpet it. I had to find superlatives I had not used before. I had to let the world know what had just happened, and in a lot of cases, what they missed.

"Michael Jordan added another page to his book of accomplishments Wednesday night and this time it came in victory instead of defeat," my story read in the newspaper the next morning.

"I got my shots off very early," Jordan said after the game. "When you are going good, everything seems to energize your game and I just tried to ride it."

Jordan told the reporters that it was his best game ever.

"This would have to be," he said.

He said something different a couple of hours later in the hotel bar of the Cleveland Airport Marriott.

When the opportunity presented itself—the opportunity being that we were in a hotel that had a bar that stayed open late enough—we reporters would often stop by the hotel bar to have a drink before going to bed. We rarely stayed up late because we usually had an early morning flight the next day to get back to Chicago or to get to our next stop on the road trip.

There was not much to promote about staying at the Cleveland Airport Marriott in the 1980s, other than the fact that it was about one minute from the airport, and it had a bar that stayed open late.

(Fun fact: one night *Tribune* writer Melissa Isaacson, *Sun-Times* writer Mike Mulligan, and I sat at the bar at the Cleveland Airport Marriott and came up with names that should have been considered for the Seven Dwarfs. Mike's favorite was "Stoolie" while I favored "Morose.")

The night of Jordan's record performance in Cleveland, the Bulls were still flying commercial, which meant that they, too, had to wait for the first flight out the next morning. So they were staying in the same hotel we were, and Jordan was apparently so jazzed by what had happened that he felt like being out.

Three reporters, including myself, were sitting in a booth in the bar when Jordan walked in alone. It was the first time I had seen him make such a public appearance late night, without a security guard with him, or at least a teammate to run interference.

He sat down with us, ordered a beer, and began to talk about the game. "Sixty-nine is a lot of points," said Jordan, who played 50 of the possible 53 minutes in the game.

He asked us what we knew about where that game ranked historically, and we told him he was 10th at the time (Bryant had not hit his 81-point game yet). We told him Wilt Chamberlain had most of the games with higher point totals than his, and he wondered how many shots Chamberlain took in those games. Since it was pre-Wi-Fi, we were unable to look up the answer immediately.

But we all knew the one fact that mattered most. Chamberlain played one game in which he scored 100 points, in which he made 36-of-63 field goals.

I asked Jordan if he thought he could ever score 100 points in a game. He thought about his answer for a few seconds.

"I don't know," he said with a sigh. "I'm pretty tired."

We all laughed. It was a rare glimpse into the human Jordan. Most people believed that Jordan could score as many points as he wanted any night he wanted. It wasn't the case. He needed overtime to get his 69.

(Quick aside: I know this joke has been used forever, but it was Stacey King who first pointed out that he and Jordan combined for 70 points in their victory over the Cavaliers that night. King contributed a single free throw to the win.)

The second time I drank with Jordan, it ended up in a legal proceeding. But I am getting ahead of myself.

The year 1988 was a very important one for the players in the NBA, because that is when the Miami Heat joined the league (Orlando joined in 1989). The city of Miami replaced Los Angeles as the party capital of the league the day the Heat played its first game. Jordan enjoyed his time in Miami a lot. He could feel the warmth of the sun he was accustomed to back home in North Carolina, he could golf during the day, and he could experience a new level of partying that topped Los Angeles and New York in many ways. Miami was something new.

While 1988 was an important year to NBA players (and the reporters who followed them), 1983 was also important, because that is the year the restaurant Hooters opened. NBA players loved Hooters.

Hooters is known for serving chicken wings in various levels of spiciness, and having them served by very attractive young women in skimpy outfits which pronounce the most appealing parts of their bodies. NBA players loved Hooters (Did I already say that? It bears repeating).

In the 1980s, Hooters was a Southern experience. They had not yet moved northward, where they perhaps would be even more appreciated in the cold-weather cities.

In 1988, Jordan was about to experience Hooters for the first time.

The hotel we stayed at in Miami was actually in the neighborhood known as Coconut Grove, and that is where the first Miami Hooters was. Our hotel was about a 100-step walk from the restaurant, which was in a two-level mall. The mall also housed a sports bar named Marino's, owned in part by Miami Dolphins quarterback Dan Marino.

On our first trip to Miami, after the game, Jordan and several players celebrated by visiting Hooters for a postgame meal. They had, in fact, already been there that afternoon for lunch. NBA players love Hooters.

In the evening gathering, I happened to be there with another reporter, and we were quickly absorbed into Jordan's group.

After the meal, Jordan wanted to go over to Marino's, which was a busy dance club after hours. But getting there was difficult, because we had to walk along the second floor balcony from one side of the mall to the other, and there were a lot of fans outside the Hooter's restaurant, waiting for Jordan to leave so they could say something to him or get a photograph or form a lasting bond.

So what we reporters and players did was form a phalanx (the only time in my life I have ever had to be in a phalanx) around Jordan to get him to the club safely. There were six of us walking around Jordan, reporters and teammates alike, acting like a security team, until we got to Marino's, which had its own security staff. They let us in, which just set off a storm of activity among the people already in the place.

During the walk to Marino's, I was punched in the face for only the second time in my life (neither of them was intentional). Somebody really wanted to touch Jordan, and was apparently going to do so whether my head was in the way or not. I took a shot across the bow, and I was not happy about it.

Once we got inside the bar, Jordan knew just what to do. He hopped over the first bar he came to, and immediately started handing out beers to anyone who wanted one. He took no money, he took no count, he just started doling out alcohol. Is that legal?

He was having the time of his life. He had the biggest smile on his face. He took a break from this behavior only to have a beer or two for himself. I admit I took advantage of his largesse.

The next day, I asked him how many beers he handed out, and he laughed. "How am I supposed to know?" he said.

Well, it turned out, Marino's knew. Or at least they had an idea. Sometime later, months maybe, the restaurant made an attempt to recoup what it lost in alcohol sales by Jordan's sudden philanthropy. I do not know how that conflict was worked out.

If they need witness corroboration, I was there.

16

Twice Quite Nice for Bulls
June 15, 1992

They made it interesting, just as they have all season long. But the Chicago Bulls finally had to cooperate with the inevitable.

Sunday, the Bulls laid claim to their second consecutive NBA world championship.

Michael Jordan scored 33 points and a squad of reserves led the Bulls back from a 17-point deficit to a 97–93 victory over the Portland Trail Blazers Sunday at Chicago Stadium.

The victory ended the 1992 NBA Finals 4–2 in the Bulls' favor, and Chicago erupted with joy, both at Chicago Stadium and in surrounding areas.

"It may not look pretty, but today we stand tall," said Jordan, who was on the bench when the Bulls made their major comeback at the start of the fourth quarter.

"We battled from behind against a very good club," said Bulls forward Scottie Pippen, who had 26 points. "Tonight was very sweet."

The Bulls were expected to win this title from Day One, but that did not take away from the pleasure of winning the second crown, even though the playoff run was much more difficult this season than last year.

"The only way for us to succeed was for us to win it all," said guard John Paxson. "It feels good to actually do it."

"We went through a lot of adversity," said Pippen, who may have been talking about both the game and the series. "It's a lot more gratifying."

There also was the team element involved, since four bench players came through with key contributions in the fourth quarter. From the starting lineup, only Pippen stood on the court at the start of the final period as the Bulls tried to erase the possibility of a Game 7 on Wednesday.

"It was a very sweet game because it was on the doorstep for us to lose," said Bulls coach Phil Jackson. "We were flirting with disaster."

Disaster was a 17-point deficit late in the third quarter. The Trail Blazers, behind 24 points from Clyde Drexler and a more impressive 22-point, six-rebound, seven-assist showing from Terry Porter, were riding as high a wave as they had enjoyed this entire series.

Almost everybody was planning schedules for a seventh game, and that seemed to include Jackson, who started the final quarter with a lineup of Pippen and four backups—B.J. Armstrong, Stacey King, Scott Williams, and Bobby Hansen. It appeared to be almost a concession to the Blazers, who had played a solid game from the start.

"We needed something different," said Jackson. "We needed kids who were fresh out there."

"I never gave up," Jordan said. "But it did look kind of dim."

But Pippen and the baby Bulls did the job and did it brilliantly. Opening with a three-point shot by Hansen at the start of the period, every one of those bench players contributed. Armstrong scored two points and handed out three assists. King scored five points, and Williams provided three rebounds in the quarter as the Bulls made their final charge.

All of this happened with Jordan, the Most Valuable Player

of the NBA Finals for the second year in a row, sitting on the bench holding his breath.

"I was just cheering for them," Jordan said. "I wasn't anxious to get in because that team had such great rhythm."

Jordan returned to the game with 8:36 remaining and his team trailing by eight points, but it was Pippen who finally managed to tie the game at 85–85 with a three-point basket. The Bulls took the lead 91–89 on another Pippen jumper with 2:21 left, perhaps ending Pippen's reputation as a big-game choker.

Paxson knocked the ball away from Porter on the next possession, and that led to a Jordan jumper, giving the Bulls their first four-point lead since they had a 4–0 edge in the game's first two minutes.

"We played a hell of a game, but it is not going to always work," said Portland coach Rick Adelman. "I was trying to stop the momentum, but we ran out of timeouts and they wouldn't let me call any more."

Extra timeouts would not have helped. The Bulls were finally ready to prove what everyone knew about them at the start of the season.

They are the best team in the NBA today.

17. Michael Jordan and the Kids

Maybe it's the smile. Maybe it's the tongue. Maybe it's the effervescence with which he played.

But Michael Jordan was always big with children. Whenever I saw Jordan in a situation where he interacted with the public, it was always about the kids.

And Jordan would seek them out. I think he always knew that adults either wanted something from him or wanted to have their picture taken with him to prove to someone else that they had "met" Jordan.

For most kids, they didn't need proof they had met Jordan. They knew in their hearts that they had. When kids tell the story of meeting Jordan, you can see it in their eyes. That was all the proof they ever needed.

At games, Jordan almost always found a moment to interact with some child on the sidelines. He also often interacted with the mascots. Especially before his first retirement, Jordan was just a big kid. In a lot of ways, he was an innocent, and in children, he saw fellow innocence. Children saw a kindred spirit, albeit one who could jump higher and run faster than they ever could. Perhaps in their dreams they were Jordan's equal.

There were two occasions that always come to mind when I think about Jordan and the kids. I was lucky to be at the right place at the right time to witness them both.

We were catching a flight out of Cleveland in the morning (it's weird that so many stories happened in either Cleveland or Denver), during those early years when the team was still flying commercial, and Jordan and I were sitting next to each other in the waiting area. We were reading a *Sports Illustrated* together (it was mine, and Jordan was reading over my shoulder). Jordan was sitting to my right; to my left was the airline counter and the window looking out at the runways.

Far to Jordan's right, in the hallway that connected all the gates, stood an African American man, his wife, and their small son. I would guess the boy was about four years old. The three of them were staring at Jordan. The boy had those wide open eyes that small children have when they see something remarkable (our eyes do not grow bigger as we get older but our faces grow, so that our big childlike eyes eventually become smaller).

I could see the three of them, but Jordan was turned toward me and the magazine and did not know he was being watched (although I assume he almost always thought he was being watched). I saw the father bend down to talk to his son, then I saw him hand the boy a pen and a piece of paper. The father was sending the boy over for an autograph (asking the boy to do the dirty work).

The boy approached slowly. Eventually, he stood near Jordan's feet, and Jordan finally saw him. The boy could not have been cuter.

Jordan turned to the boy, tilted his head, and waited.

"Are you Michael?" the boy said in a whisper.

"Yes, I'm Michael Jordan," Jordan said.

At that point, the boy was probably done. He had made contact with one of the most famous athletes in the world. They had a conversation. His life was made. He then said the only thing that came to his mind in a moment like that.

"Wow."

It was the quietest, most reverential "Wow" you could ever imagine. It conveyed exactly what "Wow" is supposed to convey: amazement and joy. The realization that something hugely significant had just taken place.

And then the boy turned and walked back to his parents. Without the autograph. In the thrill of what had just happened, he forgot to ask for the signature.

So his father sent him back. The boy ran back to Jordan, asked for the autograph, and then again walked away. The parents waved to Jordan, Jordan waved back, and we went back to reading the magazine. The second time I saw Jordan interact with a child, it was far more emotional, for me at least.

Once I became a beat writer, I became aware that Jordan's pregame ceremonies were different than that of most players. There were always a few minutes when he had something different going on, and I did not know what it was.

Eventually, I found out that before almost every game, home and road, Jordan would meet with someone who had asked for a special get-together. Make a Wish or other organizations that offer similar sorts of gifts to terminally ill children made it a habit to send someone to meet with Jordan and the best time to do it was before a game.

These meetings always took place in private. There are very few public photos of Jordan's time with those children. It was not a secret that Jordan did this, but it was never publicized. I think that was part of the deal—we will get you the meet and greet with Jordan, but keep it on the down low, because otherwise everyone will ask and everyone will be sick and dying.

We were in Los Angeles, again at the Sports Arena for a game against the Clippers, and I was making a call home in the room where Jordan was scheduled to meet with a special child and his family before the game.

Jordan always conducted these meetings with the help of one of the Bulls media relations people. I had a great relationship with those people; several of them are among my best friends in adulthood. When Jordan and the PR person walked into the room with the family, they saw me. It was Jordan who said, "You can stay," and I did, not knowing what I was about to witness.

Coming into the room with us then was a boy, a teenage boy I would guess, rather large. He was in a wheelchair, which was being driven by a man I guessed to be the boy's grandfather. Alongside him was a woman I guessed to be his mother.

The boy, who had black hair and a large oval face, was barely alive. He was seemingly incapable of movement. He raised his eyes slightly to look at Jordan, then dropped them again. His hands were still sitting on the arms of the wheelchair. His legs were large but limp. His head tilted slightly to the left, as if he could not manage to hold it up.

There was no way to know how much of the boy was left inside. He was alive only because his heart was beating.

"Thank you so much, Michael," the mother gushed. "You are his favorite player. He has posters of you all over his room."

Jordan was not dismissive of mom or grandfather; he shook hands and greeted them warmly. But his attention was entirely on the boy.

Jordan bent down and whispered to the boy. I was standing against a back wall, holding my breath. I did not hear anything that was said. Because the boy was incapable of participating in the conversation, Jordan did all the talking. And he talked quite a bit.

Eventually, the mother began to cry. In that moment, I tried to imagine what she was experiencing, and could not reach the level of emotion that she was going through. Her son, who had befallen some horrible tragedy either by birth or by incident, was meeting his favorite sports hero. During a lifetime of hurt, or perhaps even unfeeling, he was having a moment of extreme significance. If he could speak, he could probably tell his mom how amazing the entire moment was for him, and he would thank her for arranging the meeting. They would hug the hug that says it all.

But the boy was incapable of speech, and incapable of hugs. The hopelessness of the moment hit me. The boy would never be able to express his thrill for what he was experiencing, if he even knew, and he would never be able to thank Jordan or his mom. He would never be able to tell friends, cousins, or strangers about what he was experiencing, which was an event millions of other children would love to have.

I have to admit, I am an easy cry. I get choked up over life-insurance commercials. This moment, the enormous amount of emotion that was taking place among one man talking, one woman crying, and one boy sitting perfectly still, was beyond my ability to handle. I cried—quietly—but real tears ran down my face. The mom was destroying me in the crying department, but I was trying to keep up.

This went on for 10 minutes. Jordan spoke to this nearly comatose child for 10 minutes. Was there one time when the boy managed to roll his gaze up toward Jordan? Did he recognize who was speaking? Did he try to send a message through what was left of his mind?

I will never know. I think I saw him look up, but I could have imagined it through my tears. Whether Jordan felt any connection whatsoever, who knows?

After about 10 minutes, Jordan stood up. He turned to the adults and said, "Well, I've got to get ready for the game. It was nice to meet you." Then he turned to the boy and said, "Nice to meet you, too," while taking his non-responsive hand and giving it a shake.

The mother wiped away her tears and gave Jordan the biggest hug imaginable. The grandfather, himself a large man standing ramrod straight, shook Jordan's hand and looked him in the eyes as he said,

"Thank you." They turned to leave the room, and Jordan, the PR person, and I waited.

As we exited the room, I walked with Jordan back to the locker room. I had to know.

"You do something like this before almost every game, right?" I asked.

"Yeah," he said.

I must tell you that professionally, I almost always frame my questions in my head before I ask them. I am very distinct and concrete in my questioning. I want the interviewee to answer a very specific question. But in this case, I just said what came to my mouth first.

"How do you play after something like that?" I asked.

Jordan looked at me, smiled a very thin smile, shrugged, and said, "I just do." Then he walked into the locker room, and I was left to ponder what I had just witnessed.

Kids want to be great athletes because with it comes fame and fortune. People fawn all over you when you are a pro basketball or baseball or football player. You get lots of free stuff because people just want to say "Thanks" in some way.

But a lot of athletes give back, and some do it the way Jordan did it all those years.

They are not saints, but they sometimes do the work of saints. They should be recognized for doing so.

18. The Second Championship

Every year, professional sports teams like to have a slogan to use as a kind of spark, a marketing tool to differentiate one season from another. When the 1991–92 Bulls started the season going 1–2, with

Scottie Pippen hugs Horace Grant as Cliff Levingston (right) also celebrates the Bulls victory over the Trail Blazers in the 1992 NBA Finals.

losses to the Milwaukee Bucks and the Golden State Warriors, I suggested the slogan for the season should be, "Wasn't last year great?"

The Bulls then went and won 14 straight games, and everything was fine.

The second championship for the 1991–92 season was different from the first one because the final game was won in Chicago as opposed to Los Angeles. The Bulls were playing the Portland Trail Blazers, who were severely outmanned. The Bulls were deeper, Clyde Drexler was no match for Michael Jordan, and the Bulls were a steamroller as they cruised to their second title, wining the series four games to two.

In the final game, which was closer than I anticipated it would be (97–93), the initial team celebration took place in the tiny Chicago Stadium locker room. But almost immediately, coach Phil Jackson called out to the team to march back upstairs (the teams actually had to go down into the Stadium basement to reach their locker room, as did the visiting team and the officials) and celebrate with the fans, who were still screaming as they celebrated their first Bulls championship moment at home.

I'm not sure the players wanted to do it. There seemed to be some reluctance immediately. But when Jordan decided it was a good idea, everyone followed. The team was forced to celebrate with the fans, but I think they realized their more personal celebration would take place just a few minutes later than it would without the fan moment.

What happened next is well documented and can be seen on video. The players ran out onto the court, Jordan jumped up onto the scorer's table, and the fans from Chicago got to celebrate with their championship team for the first time, the way they wanted to, inside venerable Chicago Stadium. Sure, there was a Grant Park rally after the first title, just like there were after the other five, but being able to be with the team at the time of their victory, to make the rafters of that Old Barn shake, to feel the thunderous vibration of the crickety seats, it was a significant time for Chicago.

That ended up being the only Bulls championship completed at Chicago Stadium. I have always said that building made noise when it was empty; when it was filled with screaming Bulls fans, the noise was deafening. I always feared the stomping that sometimes went on, because the building was not a sturdy structure, but it held up through the party that night.

I had been in the locker room for the initial part of the celebration, and climbed back upstairs to watch the thrilling joy as the fans and the players celebrated together.

19. Shoes

NBA jerseys sell well around the world, but so do football jerseys and baseball shirts and hockey sweaters.

What sets the NBA apart in terms of equipment is the shoes.

"It's Gotta Be the Shoes" the Nike ad told us all those years ago as a way to explain what Michael Jordan was doing.

The shoes are aerodynamic but well-cushioned. They have ankle support that basketball players and hockey players need. When the NBA turned into a favored dwelling place of rock stars in the late 1980s and 1990s, the shoes started to become extremely colorful.

But they are also huge.

More than any other sport, basketball players have huge feet. There is a scientific reason for that: all of the jumping, or more specifically all of the landing, that they do on their feet push the bones out, creating larger feet.

Will Perdue, the former Vanderbilt star who came to the Bulls in the 1988 NBA draft, reportedly had size 22 shoes. At least that's what it said on the box the shoes came in. And I should know.

The Bulls were on their way to a west coast trip in Perdue's second year in the league. It was the Thanksgiving trip (known as the circus trip in Chicago because the Barnum and Bailey people take over the United Center for two weeks in November), and my wife came along for the holiday. We were leaving the day before the trip began on the

Wednesday before Thanksgiving, although the team had left the day before my wife and I did.

Which is good, because Will Perdue had forgotten something and he wanted me to bring it to him.

"Kent," he said over the phone, "I forgot my shoes. Can you carry them on the plane with you?"

Now, you would think the shoes would be something a player would pack with him. Today, in fact, the team is responsible for that vital part of the uniform, but back then the players packed both their personal and playing luggage. Somehow, the shoes skipped Perdue's mind.

But size 22 shoes are hard to ignore.

So Perdue and I arranged for me to get the shoes at O'Hare Airport. Assistant weight trainer Erik Helland, who was not on the trip, met me at the gate (back then you did not need to have a ticket to get into the gate area) and what he handed me wasn't a shoe box. It was a small refrigerator.

That's what it looked like at first. As it turns out, size 22 basketball shoes come in a box built for size 22 basketball shoes, and the box was huge. They were Nikes, and the shoe box said "Nike" all over; it was hard to miss.

Janice laughed out loud when she saw the box. So did almost everybody on the flight.

"What's in that box?" I was asked time and again. When I said, "basketball shoes," I was not believed. So I had to show them off.

Janice and I joked that we should have charged people to see them. And they were a sight to see, the largest basketball shoes I had ever seen—the largest shoes anybody on the flight had seen.

You would think that would be a once-in-a-lifetime experience, but it wasn't. A couple of years later, Horace Grant called and asked if

I could meet his wife outside the United terminal so she could give me his shoes to carry on the flight to Washington, D.C. They weren't as large, but they were still the shoes of a famed NBA basketball player. Again, I should have charged for viewings.

20. My Best Day Ever

This is a story I hoped someday would be part of a book. I always wanted to write John Paxson's memoirs. But Paxson is not the kind of guy to want to tell all of his stories, and he is not sure anyone wants to hear them, anyway. He may have a point.

But there was one day, in one particular harbor, that was actually going to be the foreword for the book I planned to write, if Paxson had just given me the go-ahead.

In 1992, after the first Bulls title, the Bulls had a road trip to Florida. They played the Orlando Magic on a Saturday, then flew to Miami, where they did not play until Monday night. There was no practice scheduled on Sunday, so that gave the team and those who followed it all day Sunday to play.

The team had the day off, and I had pre-written a feature for Sunday so I could have as much time to myself as possible in the warmest place the league and the newspaper would send me. Paxson and I agreed we would find someplace outdoors to sit and have a lengthy lunch, which would include many beers.

So, at right about noon on that Sunday, we found a place to eat. It was at the corner of Walk and Don't Walk (who knows the real street names) and it offered peel 'em shrimp and beers, both by the bucket. For two confirmed Parrotheads, it was the perfect way to waste away.

Bulls' assistant trainer Erik Helland was with us, and the weather was perfect. We could have stayed there all day. As a matter of fact, we did. It was 9:00 PM when we finally left our table, and went out to do something else fun.

At one point during that lunch that lasted forever, we started up a conversation with a young couple sitting near us. I remember that the woman's name was Mary. She and her male companion were of Latin descent. They asked us why we were in Miami. I told them we were with the Chicago Bulls, and Mary and her boyfriend knew of the Chicago Bulls.

"Oh, Michael Jordan!" she said, displaying the one absolute fact she had at her disposal regarding the Bulls. "Are you players?"

Paxson, at 6'2", was not obviously a basketball player, because he was not close to 7" tall or African American, so we gave her a break with the question. At this point, I took up the conversation with Mary, because Paxson is shy.

"John is a player," I said. "In fact, he is an important player. Do you know anything about basketball?"

"Yes, a little," Mary said.

"Okay," I said. "What position does Michael Jordan play?"

And Mary said, "He's a dribbler."

That was Mary's way of saying that Jordan played the guard position. If you don't know the word "guard" then "dribbler" would suffice.

"And how many dribblers are there on a team?" I asked her.

"Two," she said.

And I pointed to John and said, "He's the other dribbler."

And from that point on and all the way to today, that is the name of the unwritten memoirs of John Paxson—The Other Dribbler.

21. The Phone Call

Ispent a lot of time in my life wondering what it would be like to be Michael Jordan. I could definitely handle the task of being incredibly wealthy; I have been ready for that for years. And I think I could handle the fame; I would just run away from it if it became necessary.

I'm sure there are bad parts. It became well known that when Jordan would want to go shopping, he would have someone call store management (or sometimes mall management) and arrange for the stores to stay open past their usual closing time so he could shop in peace. He had a hard time living anything that resembles a normal life.

It's hard for him to go anywhere without being noticed, and with notice often comes the approach, the request for photos and signatures, and even more. There is very little in the way of privacy. Moments we all take for granted are precious or even passed over because Jordan was too famous to do them.

Which brings to mind the one Saturday in 1990 when Jordan called me at home.

On the previous Friday, I had called Jordan to ask him something for an upcoming story. I never actually got him on the phone; I always had to leave a message and he would call back. For some reason, he thought it would be a good idea to call me at 7:30 AM on a Saturday morning to a household without kids. Needless to say, my wife, Janice, and I were asleep when the phone rang.

The phone was on Janice's side of the bed, and she picked it up.

"Hello?" she said in a morning voice that probably had a hint of annoyance in it.

"May I speak to Kent, please?" the voice on the other end said.

"May I ask who is calling?" Janice asked.

"It's Michael Jordan," Jordan replied.

At which Janice handed the phone over to me and said, "He *says* it's Michael Jordan." As if to suggest she thought it was some friend pulling a prank.

I put the phone to my ear and heard Jordan laughing hard.

"Sorry about that," I said.

"I get that all the time," he said.

22. Playing the Game

My first NBA game as a reporter was covering the Indiana Pacers as the state sports editor for United Press International in Indianapolis. It was 1980; the Pacers still had George McGinnis and Billy Knight and Mickey Johnson. They also had a young James Edwards, who one day would be a backup center for the Chicago Bulls.

The Pacers were only a few years removed from being in the American Basketball Association before it folded and four teams from the ABA joined the NBA. (For the record, and for the unending pleasure of my sons, it is important that you know the four were the Pacers, the San Antonio Spurs, the Denver Nuggets, and the New York Nets.)

I grew up in Indianapolis, in a south suburb named Beech Grove. Growing up in Indiana taught me that high school basketball was the breeding ground for the greatest level of basketball, which was the college game. Nothing, not one thing, could replace the value of high school basketball and the quality of college basketball.

Once players got to the National Basketball Association, what was being played more closely resembled the Harlem Globetrotters than what was considered real basketball. It is in that culture I was raised, and those feelings remained with me as I covered by first NBA game.

I will never understand "continuation." Who thought that was a good idea? It wasn't somebody who understood the significance of fouling a player on the floor so that his shot does not count; he would be shooting a one-and-one or perhaps not shooting free throws at all, as opposed to what happens as a result of continuation, which is going to the line for sure for either an and-one or two free tosses.

At the time of my first Pacers game, I was still getting accustomed to sitting as close as I did to the floor. The college games I covered at Indiana and Purdue had me sitting up in the stands; the NBA allowed us floor-level seating (although they are taking that away all across the league now to make room for $800 courtside seats).

I was seated next to a colleague from the Associated Press, a guy who had been around the block. He was extremely considerate of my youth and my relative inexperience, and explained quite a few things to me as we went along in that game.

The best example was when a ridiculously bad call was made against the Pacers at the far end of the floor, and when the teams played directly in front of us, there was another bad call that went in the Pacers' favor.

"Mascara," my colleague said.

I looked at him quizzically.

"That was a make-up call," he said. "The refs blew the call on one end, so they come down and make another bad call to make up for the first one."

And the reality of the pro game became obvious to me.

Certainly, make-up calls are difficult to watch. Fans don't always know that they even exist, and they just think a bad refereeing crew makes two bad calls in a row. Instead, the refs are doing what they have apparently done forever, and balance the fates when they can as part of the "show" that is the NBA.

When I started covering the Bulls several years later, I got accustomed to the idea that the referees would give Jordan the benefit of the doubt more often than not. The league not only protects its superstars, it promotes them. I would not disagree with a statistic that showed that the top players in the league get an extra 10 points per game as a result of phantom calls on drives to the hoop, or touch fouls that would otherwise go uncalled.

That's where continuation comes in again. A superstar who is fouled on the floor knows that he can go ahead and "make" the basket, knowing that it will count and he will get the extra free throw when in fact his team should probably just be running an inbounds play. Completely irritating to me; I even play Monopoly by the rules in the book.

For the most part, the other players know this is going to happen. They will complain, perhaps, but only for a short moment. They know they aren't going to get the call reversed, and complaining just riles up the referee to make the same sort of call again later in the game.

I did not like that aspect of the game. I tolerated it. But I suffered through it. A foul is a foul, no matter who commits it. Conversely, a player going to the rim who is not touched is not fouled.

John Paxson, who eventually became one of my best friends, hated the phantom calls. He would usually get visually upset by them when they were called against him, mainly because he tried to take advantage of the proper technique of fouling the guy on the floor so that he doesn't get credit for the ensuing shot. He, like many others before and after him, was brought up with the rules of the game as played at the high school and college level and bristled at the unspoken NBA rules.

But the players are in on it. They know they all benefit from a game that has superstars. They know that they are all in this together, for the most part. While team rivalries exist, player rivalries are fading, because they are all on one big corporate, money-making ride and their uniforms just happen to be what they are wearing that particular day.

There is a great deal of in-game conversation that takes place as players from opposing teams talk about the refs, their coaches, their teammates, or cheerleaders. When you sit as close as I did all those years, you see a lot of stuff that fans think they would like to see, but which actually takes away from the image of the game as pure competition.

The best example from my years was in a game between the Bulls and the Dallas Mavericks in Dallas. The Bulls had the ball with 15 seconds left in the first half, and they were going to run an isolation play for Michael Jordan, as they had done thousands of times before.

You have seen the play, if not run by Jordan then run by most point guards in the league. The player with the ball employs a standing dribble between the circles until the clock runs down to a certain second, and then they run their play.

On this day in Dallas, Jordan was facing longtime opponent Derek Harper of the Mavericks. Jordan started his standing dribble with about 13 seconds remaining, and Harper said to him, "When do you go?" which meant "At one point on the clock will you begin the play?"

For that brief moment, I thought, *What a weird question. Why would Jordan tell his opponent when he would make his move to begin the play for a final shot at the basket?*

But you know what happened? Jordan answered him.

"Seven," Jordan said.

And sure enough, when the clock wound down to seven seconds remaining, Jordan ran the play, dribbling to his left with his left hand, crossing over right as Harper leaned too far to his own right, and hitting the 14-foot jumper that sent the Bulls into the locker room with two extra points.

I always marveled at that moment. That kind of sharing would never have gone over well at any of the levels of basketball below the NBA. But in the pros, perhaps it doesn't matter what your opponent knows. They still have to be able to stop the play, and with Jordan at the helm, they often could not.

23. On Top of the Game

Since the Bulls won their last championship in 1998, the NBA has gone through a process of removing the media from some of their access to the players. Unlike when I got started and the Bulls were working out in front of club members at the public gym facility known as the Deerfield Multiplex, practices today are held in private buildings constructed for the use of the team, and practices are closed to the view of outsiders. The team often decides which player addresses the media after practice. There is absolutely no attempt to force the players to talk to the media after games. Often, the stars of the game make the reporters wait half an hour after the game before making themselves available for interviews, which messes with deadlines, for reporters who still have deadlines.

I never understand why players would make reporters wait like that. It was always my contention that if the players talked when the locker room opened up 10 minutes after the game, reporters would get their quotes and sound bites and leave. The locker room would then be a safe haven for the players to talk about the game, or their postgame plans, or the upcoming road trip, or about which reporter they hate the most. We would be gone.

Instead, they play this weird waiting game with reporters, perhaps to see how many will wait and put themselves in danger of missing deadline in order to get that one sentence that might actually help their story. It's a power play, and it is annoying and childish.

The other way that the NBA has removed the media from proximity to the players and the game is by moving media row from courtside along the length of the court to courtside behind the baskets and in some cases even off the floor. True, there are a lot more media to accommodate, but even the beat writers find themselves removed in some cities so that the teams can sell that space as a seat to a paying customer who sometimes comes close to paying four digits for that seat.

Which is all okay by me.

When I was a beat writer, I was on TV all the time. I was sitting courtside and the players would walk past me on the way to enter the game and I was there, doing my job. In some cases, I am famously right there.

When Michael Jordan hit the game-winner over Craig Ehlo of the Cleveland Cavaliers in that playoff series before the Bulls started winning championships, and the camera pans to coach Doug Collins exploding off the bench to celebrate the series win, I am right there, writing down some significant fact for my story later.

When Horace Grant blocked Kevin Johnson to preserve the Bulls' 1993 championship against the Phoenix Suns, I am right there, in plain view of the most often-used video clip, with my arms folded across my chest as I prepared to write my third NBA championship story.

But there were a lot of times I did not like being that close to the action.

I hated games in New York. The Bulls and Knicks really hated each other, and those games were always brutally physical. I was always concerned that a major fight would break out; I was always watchful that I did not end up in one of the fights that breached the confines of the basketball playing area and worked its way up into the audience.

I had Patrick Ewing fall on me once. I had Charles Barkley slide into my seat behind the basket. In Detroit, I thought Bill Laimbeer was going to take real offense to my position courtside as he tried to save a ball that was going out of bounds.

Seats that close to the action are good for getting the small details of the game, but working conditions are not the best. Plus, you hear every word said behind you as fans turn ugly and scream and shout at the opposing team.

No place was worse than Philadelphia. The City of Brotherly Love has a reputation for having the worst fans in all of American sports, and it is well-deserved. Those scenes from the movie *Invincible* in which the fans were willing to abuse actress Elizabeth Banks for wearing a New York Giants jersey were representative.

I mean, who would want to hurt Elizabeth Banks?

In one game in Philadelphia's old Spectrum, I was seated behind the basket just off the floor, and Mike Mulligan of the *Sun-Times* was seated to my left. Behind us was a fan, a large man, who made it quite clear that he did not like Michael Jordan or the Bulls.

His screams were mean-spirited and irritating, and Mulligan and I were both amused and offended by some of his remarks. But when he jumped out of his seat, and leaned over our shoulders to get as close as he could to Jordan to express one incoherent point, I thought he and Mulligan were going to have a go.

Honestly, there is such a thing as being too close to the action.

It's kind of irritating these days to listen to some game broadcasts. In some arenas, while the visiting TV crews get floor seats, the visiting radio broadcasters are put a level or even two above the floor, and they make it quite clear they are not where they want to be. However, they actually can see the game better from up above; they just don't get to enjoy the player interaction they get courtside.

24. Horace

Horace Grant came to the Bulls as a country-bumpkin type of ball player. Born in Georgia, he came to adulthood in South Carolina, and he was an uncomplicated guy. He was also fully aware of who he was in the Bulls hierarchy.

He wanted to be the third star on what would become a championship team, and he struggled when stardom did not come to him.

He received the nickname "The General" from his defensive-minded coach Johnny Bach for his stalwart efforts defending bigger power forwards. Eventually, Grant grew into his role both physically and emotionally, as the player most likely to be found in the weight room and the player most likely to wonder why the world wasn't paying him proper homage.

He struggled with the lack of notoriety as fans began to notice what Scottie Pippen could do as Robin to Michael Jordan's Batman. Did Grant want to be Batgirl? Probably not, but he wanted to be seen as an equal among stars (something that did happen for Dennis Rodman when he took Grant's place as starting power forward for the second three-peat).

When the Bulls finally made the NBA Finals in 1991, Grant spoke to me about his role on the team and coming to grips with what the NBA and the outside world thought of him.

"I don't get much recognition, but I've lived with it for four years and it doesn't bother me," Grant said. "I've accepted my role. I'm at

Bill Cartwright and Stacey King chat as Horace Grant is interviewed at the Multiplex in Deerfield, Illinois, in 1992.

peace with myself. The recognition is not there, but as long as we win, that's what counts."

Grant was also fully aware that so much of the fame he did receive was a result of having Phil Jackson as coach. Grant was not a great quote, but I remember this conversation very well because of how directly he stated his belief that Jackson was responsible for so much of the Bulls' success.

"Phil is really the key behind all this we've done as a team," Grant said. "Phil is more of a teacher than a coach. He understands when you make a mistake. If Phil would walk into my house with encyclopedias,

I'd buy every one. He's like a father figure out there, a real players' coach. He's made me better by just teaching the game."

Grant and Scottie Pippen were drafted in the same year, 1987, and because they both had humble country beginnings, they became fast friends. That friendship began to suffer a bit when Pippen became a superstar and Grant did not, but they remained close friends the entire time they played together, until Grant left the team in 1994.

While the relationship grew a bit chillier off the floor eventually, it warmed up on the floor, as Jackson taught them the significance of playing together. It was really visible to those of us who were with them every day; Pippen and Grant grew up in front of us and became professional basketball players.

"Scottie and Horace came in together as rookies and were like puppies roaming around," Jackson said.

"It was a frivolous atmosphere surrounding them. Now they're always getting together and figuring what they want to do out on the floor. That's maturity."

There was one other thing about Grant that made him a favorite of reporters. While he wanted recognition, he did not let his disappointment at being a third banana affect his relationship with the media. Until the spring of 1993, when Jordan pulled away from reporters because of the gambling story that surrounded him, and Pippen and Grant withdrew as well in a show of support for their teammate, Grant was always available for a quote after practice or after a game.

In fact, he was almost too accommodating.

I actually witnessed this after one game. A reporter came up to Grant and asked him why the Bulls had played lackluster defense for most of the game (even though they won). Grant answered something like, "Sometimes you can't give your full defensive effort in every game."

Then, just a couple of minutes later, a different reporter came up with the belief that the Bulls won that particular game because of their defense, and asked Grant if he agreed.

"Yeah," Grant said. "Sometimes you are going to have difficulty scoring, but defense will always be there if you are willing to give the effort."

That's accommodating, is what that is.

25. The Twins

One night during the playoffs in 1989, we were getting ready for a game at the Chicago Stadium. For some reason, while all of his teammates were getting dressed or taped, Horace Grant was sitting in his locker, wearing a crisp manila suit with a robin's egg blue shirt and shiny sunglasses. Horace just sat there, not talking, while his teammates got dressed for the game. People started calling him "Hollywood Horace" because of the glasses and the outfit.

Coach Doug Collins walked in, saw Grant sitting at his locker still in street clothes, and said, "If you don't want to play, we'll just start Jack [Haley]."

Then assistant coach Tex Winter asked Horace to sign a souvenir basketball.

One problem…it wasn't Horace.

It was his twin brother, Harvey, who played for the Washington Bullets and had just concluded his season.

In 1989, the two were very identical, but by the time Grant left the Bulls after the 1994 season, he had built himself up to such strength through the Bulls' weight training staff that he had outgrown his brother. While Horace played power forward his entire career, Harvey ended up being a small forward and did not have as long a career.

26. The Third Championship

The third championship was a special one for me. It was the one the Bulls were not supposed to win.

Perhaps it is wrong to say that winning gets old, but it sure can make you old.

The Bulls were exhausted when they played the 1992–93 season. There was a great deal of unhappiness. Scottie Pippen and Horace Grant, the No. 2 and No. 3 stars on the team, were complaining about their contracts. John Paxson was having knee problems and B.J. Armstrong was chomping at the bit to get more playing time at point guard. Bill Cartwright, who was old when he joined the Bulls in 1988, was even older by 1992.

Two years of going to the finals, followed by two summers of adulation and parties and celebrations, had taken its toll on the Bulls.

They went 57–25 and swept the Atlanta Hawks and Cleveland Cavaliers in the first two rounds of the playoffs. They had a bitter battle with the New York Knicks in the Eastern Conference Finals, winning that series 4–2. Then they had to face the Phoenix Suns, who had the best record in the league that year at 62–20. The Suns had homecourt advantage in the series.

The Bulls won the first two championships by being superior to their opponents in almost every way. The Suns, however, came in with a weapon the Bulls would have difficulty dealing with, the top scoring offense in the league. They were averaging 113 points per game!

The Bulls had a 3–2 lead in the series heading into Game 6, but they were going back to Phoenix for the final two games. The Suns knew if they could win Game 6, they would host Game 7, and winning a seventh game in a championship series as the road team is very difficult in the NBA.

The Bulls had also developed a history of avoiding seven-game series. Only the conference semifinals in 1992 had gone to the last possible game, when the Bulls beat the New York Knicks soundly 110–81 in one of the most punishing playoff series of my memory.

The Suns were not going to get to host a Game 7, however, because John Paxson hit that jumper with seconds left in the game, and Horace Grant blocked Kevin Johnson's runner in the lane to seal the outcome.

Paxson had played so deeply in the shadow of Jordan, Pippen, and Grant, that it was thrilling to see him finally have his day in the sun. Paxson and I had developed a friendship over the years, one that has lasted well past his playing time and my beat-writer career, and I probably had never been so happy for a friend in my life.

In fact, if you watch the video of Johnson's shot that Grant blocked to complete the victory, you will see a man on press row in a white shirt with a black tie and his arms crossed on his chest. In the most-watched video, you cannot see the man's head; the shot angle is lower. But that man is me. When Paxson hit that shot, I wrote down the time, then crossed my arms because I knew my friend had just won the NBA title for the Chicago Bulls. And I was correct.

In the locker room (a much more modern locker room, by the way, than the first two titles; the America West Arena was brand new in 1993), the NBA handed out the championship trophy for the third time in three years to the Chicago Bulls. Only this time, my good friend

John Paxson was on the stage, and he looked out at me amongst the crowd and mouthed the words, "I'm the goods."

That was the first time I was staying in the same hotel as the team. We were in the Phoenix Ritz Carlton, and the place was buzzing all night long. There were many rumors about the behavior that night.

Johnny "Red" Kerr, a Chicago native who became the Bulls' first coach in the 1960s and eventually their longtime color commentator on television, sat down with me in the lobby after the game. No one was going to sleep, certainly not Johnny, who liked to party as much as any of the younger Bulls staffers.

"We really have to enjoy this," Kerr said. "We are never going to see another team like this. No one is ever going to win the way this team has."

He had a point. He was wrong, in turned out, but he had a point. It was important to cherish what the Bulls had done, and it was equally important for the Bulls fans to appreciate what they were in the midst of.

27. My First and Only Practical Joke

I don't like practical jokes. They are harmful. They can have unseen unpleasant consequences. They do not elicit laughs as much as they do gasps. "I can't believe you did that!" is more often than not a declaration that follows news of an effective practical joke.

I am, in fact, afraid of being the butt of a practical joke. I suppose I will always have that fear in the back of my mind.

My dislike for practical jokes makes this story all the more unusual. I pulled off a doozy, one that ended up all the way in the office of NBA commissioner David Stern.

In the spring of 1993, as the Bulls were marching to their third NBA title, Michael Jordan was under intense media scrutiny for allegations of gambling misbehaviors. He was accused of gambling large sums of money playing golf, which is not illegal. But the amounts that were rumored were staggering, and Jordan was not enjoying himself.

As a result, Jordan withdrew from the media. As the playoffs began, and dozens of reporters would gather at the Bulls practice facility, the Berto Center, for quotes to fill stories in between games, Jordan would not accommodate. Seeing that Jordan was allowed to avoid the media, Scottie Pippen and Horace Grant soon joined suit. Veterans John Paxson and Bill Cartwright were still available, but Cartwright was not a good quote, and eventually Paxson got tired of being the only guy who was talking.

The NBA felt like it had to do something to placate the media, so it did. It fined the Bulls $25,000 for not forcing the players to make themselves available to the media. During that playoff run, the NBA fined the Bulls more than once for that indiscretion.

I was not upset by the dismissive behavior of the players. I have been mistreated and disregarded as a media member more times than I can count and certainly more times than I choose to remember. As long as the players weren't picking and choosing who they would talk to, as long as all of us reporters were in the same boat, I was okay with it.

But some reporters were very offended, and some were adamant that the Bulls were being childish and spoiled and should be punished more than they were. When the Bulls played the New York Knicks in the NBA Eastern Conference Finals and were fined a second time for the same indiscretion, some reporters were demanding the league do something more dramatic to enforce the need to address the media.

We were in New York before one of the games in that intense, hateful series, and I was having a pregame meal with about eight other reporters in the back rooms of Madison Square Garden. Among the people at our table was a female reporter who had covered the NBA for years, and she would not stop talking about the Bulls and their media brush-off.

I had known this woman for several years, and I knew her to be rather humorless in her approach to the game and to her job. That's not a sin, but it did run counter to my belief that while it was important to do our jobs to the best of our abilities, we were still covering a game. It was not life or death. Her unrelenting pursuit of justice in the matter of the leagues' interview process finally got the best of me.

Something in me snapped, and I, for the only time in my life that I can remember, thought I would rouse some rabble.

"I don't know for a fact that this is true, but someone in the Bulls' organization told me the team isn't even paying the fines issued by the league," I said, making sure my female colleague could hear me. "The league announces the fines, but they don't expect the Bulls to pay up. It's all just for show and public relations purposes."

"Really? Are you sure?" she asked. She was aghast at the mere suggestion that this might be true. But she also knew I was fairly well plugged into the Bulls, and she certainly had no reason to think I was lying. And I wasn't lying; I was fabricating. After a career as a non-fiction writer, I was expanding my boundaries professionally.

And, as soon as that conversation was over, I forgot about it. I enjoyed the fact that she was so up in arms, but I never gave it another thought after I cleaned up my dishes from the meal.

Two days later, I was in my hotel room in New York preparing for the next game in the series, when I got a call from Brian McIntyre, who at the time was the head of the NBA's media relations team and today is senior communications advisor to the commissioner of the league. He had been the head of the Bulls media relations staff when I started covering the team before he moved to the league office, and we had a terrific relationship.

From the moment McIntyre spoke to me that morning, I feared I might have negatively affected that relationship, though I had no idea how. He did not sound happy.

"What did you do?" McIntyre said. There was no anger in his voice, but there was a sense of immediacy.

"What are you talking about?" I asked, and I really had no idea what was coming next.

"What did you tell [the woman reporter] about the Bulls and their fines?" he said.

And I started to laugh. And McIntyre started to laugh.

So I explained what I had done, and I told him that A) I admitted at the time I had no proof and B) I said it as just an aside to a conversation, and did not push or promote the story in any way. I did not put it in my newspaper, mainly because it was complete fiction, thought up by me in a moment of weakness. I told McIntyre I just made it up.

"Well, she took it all the way to the commissioner," McIntyre said. "She is demanding answers."

And I laughed again. And I laughed after I got off the phone.

I'm laughing now.

28

Third Title Is In the Books
June 21, 1993

PHOENIX—Making history is supposed to be difficult, or everybody would do it.

The Bulls, exhausted from three years of championship basketball, were up to the task Sunday and are now this generation's greatest basketball team.

Michael Jordan scored 33 points and his career-long teammate John Paxson made a three-pointer with 3.9 seconds remaining, lifting the Bulls to a heart-pounding 99–98 victory over the Phoenix Suns to clinch their third consecutive NBA championship.

Not since the Boston Celtics of almost 30 years ago has a team won three straight NBA crowns.

"This championship meant a lot to me personally because winning three in a row is something that Larry Bird and Magic Johnson and Isiah Thomas weren't able to do," said Jordan, who won his third consecutive Finals MVP award. "We may not know what it means now but when our kids get bigger and other people have their kids and we remember this day, that is going to bring a proud smile to anybody's face."

The Los Angeles Lakers and Detroit Pistons both failed in their attempts to win a third consecutive championship during the 1980s.

The Bulls, who lost two of three games at home in this series, had to win their third consecutive game at the Suns' home stadium, the America West Arena, in order to claim the historic title.

Charles Barkley and Dan Majerle each scored 21 points for the Suns, who had a 98–94 lead with 2:23 left but failed to score again after forcing the series back to Phoenix with their two wins in Chicago last week.

"I didn't get what I wanted, and my team didn't get what it wanted," Barkley said. "At times like this it's bad to be an athlete. You want to say it was a great year, but you feel so bad right now."

Scottie Pippen scored 23 points. B.J. Armstrong had 18 points with four three-pointers, and Horace Grant made up for another poor performance with a huge last-second block, proving the Bulls are indeed a complete team, now one for the history books.

"It took a great team effort from the coaches as well as the players," Armstrong said. "This one means more to me than the other two because we had to work more as a team."

The Suns, making their first Finals appearance since 1976, were quiet in defeat but were uncertain they had been beaten by a better team.

"We beat them in every area of the game but the final score," said Phoenix coach Paul Westphal. "I told the team after the game they had a fine season and they were still a great team; they just lost to a great team tonight."

Paxson, the 10-year pro whose career is nearing its end, added to his remarkable history as a Bull by nailing the three-pointer on a pass from Horace Grant on what they knew was their last play of the game.

"I've caught the ball and shot it like that my whole life," Paxson said. "When it left my hand it felt good. There was no one around me, so I really got a good look."

It was Paxson who hit five three-pointers in the fourth quarter of Game 5 in Los Angeles two years ago, helping the Bulls earn title No 1.

Sunday's thrilling final basket was necessary only because the Bulls were unable to get any offense going in the fourth quarter.

Taking a comfortable 87–79 lead into the final period, the Bulls did not score for the first 6:09 of the period, allowing the Suns to battle to an 88–88 tie with 5:34 remaining.

"We let their pressure run us out of our offense," Pippen said "We got too erratic. We should have settled down."

Jordan was the only Bull who could contribute offensively, getting all of the Bulls' points until Paxson's bomb.

The Suns led 98–94 when Frank Johnson missed a jumper and Jordan got the rebound, went the length of the court, and made a layup with 38 seconds remaining. Majerle missed a jumper with 13.6 seconds left for Phoenix, setting up the final Bulls' run.

After Paxson's shot, there were still 3.9 seconds left on the clock at that point and the Bulls needed one more stop. After two timeouts, one by each team, the Suns ran a play with Kevin Johnson attempting a shot from just outside the free-throw line. But Grant blocked the shot from behind after letting K.J. slip past him, and the victory was sealed.

As a precursor to the final shot, the Bulls used the three-pointer effectively in the first quarter, making 5-of-6 bombs to build a 37–28 lead. Jordan had three three-pointers and Armstrong two in the first 12 minutes.

The Suns forced two ties in the second quarter but never

led and the Bulls had a 56–51 lead at halftime. They stretched the lead to 10 points on several occasions in the third quarter and got a jumper from Trent Tucker to complete the third period with an 87–79 lead.

29. Jordan and Cartwright

Michael Jordan and Bill Cartwright did not have a lot in common. Jordan played guard, Cartwright played center. Jordan was smooth, Cartwright was, well, whatever the opposite of smooth is. Jordan liked to talk. Cartwright liked to think.

Jordan did not tolerate centers gladly. They were mostly in the way. It is hard to say that Jordan was ever extremely close with any of the centers he played with during the championship years, but Cartwright was at the bottom of that list.

Cartwright was the guy the Bulls got when general manager Jerry Krause traded Jordan's very good friend Charles Oakley to New York, and Jordan resented Cartwright for that from Day One.

The two rarely spoke to each other. They were also reluctant to say nice things about each other.

But Michael Jordan and Bill Cartwright had one thing in common: They liked playing day games.

Day games are usually played on Sundays after the National Football League season is over and the NBA might be able to get some notice. Only the best teams are invited to play on Sunday afternoon, because it is still Sunday afternoon, after all, and that is usually considered family time.

Sunday afternoon usually follows Saturday night, and since teams never play both Saturday night and Sunday afternoon, players would have a Saturday night off. Calling them in for an early appearance at the stadium on Sunday morning is a test for some players in that situation, especially the young ones.

But both Jordan and Cartwright said they were ready to go around lunch time.

"I like playing this time of day," Jordan once told me in preparation for a day game. "I like getting straight out of bed and playing, then having the rest of the day off. I don't know if they [his teammates] like it, though."

"I think we should play all of our games at this time," Cartwright said after a different 1:00 PM start. "Why don't we play all of our games in the afternoon?"

Cartwright was serious with his question. I told him fans who work during the week can't make afternoon games Monday through Friday. But it was never about the fans with Cartwright, who just shrugged his shoulders when I explained the situation to him.

Jordan did not need Cartwright's approval for anything, and Cartwright was rarely asked about Jordan. But Jordan was asked about Cartwright all the time, because everyone knew they weren't best buddies.

In private, Jordan was dismissive of Cartwright. But eventually, as they started winning titles together, Jordan was publicly aware that Cartwright needed to get some props from him.

"I questioned that trade a lot before," Jordan said after the first title. "But I'm not now."

30

Finally, Jordan Can Just Be Mike
October 7, 1993

Being Michael Jordan, while probably a joy on payday, must be an awesome proposition on other days.

On Wednesday, being Michael Jordan became a little easier to handle.

Jordan's decision to retire from the NBA comes as a surprise but not a shock. What's shocking is that Jordan would ever consider coming back.

Think about what it must be like to be Michael Jordan. At home, it's probably a cushy existence, although it is also occasionally mundane, as home life almost always is.

But in public, being Michael Jordan has got to be a struggle. Being fawned over and adored has its merits, so I'm told, but being pawed and grabbed and crowded and cornered and confined in the loneliness of a hotel suite is not a pleasant way to live.

While plying his trade with the Bulls, Jordan was his most visible, most examined, most pressured. He put up with the claustrophobic atmosphere of a hotel room, albeit plush, and the hassle of entering and exiting stadiums through crowds of fans who want a piece of him.

It was the 48 minutes on the floor every night that held him together through all of that push and pull. For nine years, he played harder than any other athlete, willed bad teams to win occasionally and a good team to win three consecutive titles.

He considered retirement after the first title, was urged to

Bulls players, coaches, and front office staff look on during Michael Jordan's retirement press conference.

give it up by family and friends. But he was not done proving himself. Last summer he was exhausted from the Dream Team experience and two NBA title runs. Bulls coach Phil Jackson had to talk him out of retiring then, telling him that only a third title could lift his legend above that of Magic Johnson, Larry Bird, and Isiah Thomas.

So he pulled himself and the team through that silly regular season and on to a third title.

Jackson tried to promote the idea that the three-time champion Bulls have not received their due, that no one in the NBA community believes those teams comprise a dynasty. He hoped that topic would fire the nearly endless competitive imagination of Jordan.

Then he hit upon the one personal goal Jordan could possibly have, knowing Jordan was tied with Wilt Chamberlain with seven consecutive scoring titles, Jackson told Jordan to use the chase for an eighth such title as an incentive for 1993–94.

Perhaps, under normal circumstances, Jordan would have fallen for those ruses. But the death of James Jordan clouded the horizon.

Michael Jordan suffered an immense emotional loss, one that left him drained for weeks. He could not even find solace in golf, his newest competitive passion.

There was a psychological toll, certainly, but there was a physical one as well. A man who was already physically exhausted became more so due to a personal tragedy.

Jordan could have played this season in honor of his father, but it would have been a hollow and public display of affection. Instead, Jordan chose to pull away from his public self.

His work is done, and who is going to tell him to go back to the grindstone? Not me, that's for sure.

Watching Michael Jordan perform his magic has been a great thrill for me. One that I will describe to my children and grandchildren, perhaps to the point of irritation.

But attempting to document the legend of Michael Jordan has been a tiring process.

Being the legend Michael Jordan has got to be indescribably exhausting.

Now he can rest.

31. Pippen's Hall of Fame Status

We were in the locker room in Seattle one year, and I sat down to talk to Pippen. It was during the time Jordan was first retired, and Pippen was weary of trying to carry the team on his back.

The thing about Pippen that always made him a favorite is that he was unassuming. It took him a long time to realize he was a star in the league. He knew he would always take a back seat to Jordan, and he was mostly okay with it. But he knew he also was never going to get a fair shake as long as that comparison was dogging him.

Scottie dunks on Craig Ehlo in the 1993 Eastern Conference Semifinals. *(Photo courtesy Getty Images)*

He knew his statistics would always be compared to Jordan, which he didn't mind so much when it came to points. But he also knew, eventually, that he was a better defensive player than Jordan, and so he would occasionally look at the final box score and shake his head when he looked at the steals numbers.

"You know," he told me, "if I tap the ball away from a player and Michael picks it up, he gets the steal. And if he taps the ball away and I pick it up, he gets the steal."

But in Seattle that day, he was contemplating his place in history, and showed me a bit of surprising respect because he wanted my opinion on something.

"Do you think I'll make the Hall of Fame?" he asked.

I told him, "Yes."

I didn't tell him that my rule is that whenever someone asks me if they are going to get into the Hall of Fame I always say "yes."

32. Michael Jordan Returns

"I'm back."

With those two words, issued in the form of a press release faxed to everyone that might want to know, Michael Jordan let the world know he was returning to the NBA. It was March of 1995, and Jordan was going to reinsert himself in the league and into the team with one month left to prepare himself for the NBA playoffs.

As it turned out, it wasn't enough. Jordan was only a shadow of his former self in that month-plus, and his performance in the second-round playoff series against the Orlando Magic was depressing.

During his time away from basketball, I had almost no contact with him. He sought me out once at the Chicago Stadium when he returned for a game, but he was just using me for cover from other members of the media who were trying to get him to talk about his baseball career. In all of the time I knew Jordan and had a phone number to reach him, I think I dialed the number only three times.

That may be why he seemed not to mind me being around. I didn't bother him unless it was absolutely necessary.

One morning while Jordan was retired from basketball, I returned on a flight from Charlotte to O'Hare Airport. I was outside waiting for a cab to pick me up and take me home. There was a black sedan parked along the same aisle, and it had dark-tinted windows. Suddenly, one of the windows rolled down.

"Hey, Kent," Jordan called out from the car.

He was waiting for his mother who, unbeknownst to me, was on my flight. We talked a little about baseball, a little about the Bulls, we laughed over a couple of things, and then Deloris showed up.

Once Jordan returned to basketball, but before the summer of 1995 when he actually took the time to get himself back into basketball shape, he had very little exposure, very little contact with the media. He was definitely more guarded after going through the inquisition he faced over his gambling habits, and the horrible tragedy that befell him when his father was murdered.

But I did have one moment in the spring of 1995 with him which I wrote about and got a good deal of attention for.

I have a bit of a personal problem, although it is not a problem for me. I like to be early. To everything. If I am on time, I feel like I am late. My kids and wife hate it, but it serves me well. I have extra time to get acclimated to wherever I am ending up, and I rarely have to worry about ever actually being late.

Long before the Bulls were winning championships, Jordan had stopped going onto the court to take pregame warm-up shots. His presence was too distracting to the other players trying to warm up and everybody in the stands called his name, begging for attention. It was part of the price he paid for his enormous fame.

Before one game in the spring of 1995, I happened to be at the United Center early, well before fans were allowed into the building, and I went out to the court. There was Jordan, hanging on the rim of the west-side basket.

"What are you doing?" I said, in an incredulous voice.

He let go of the rim and called me over.

"This rim is tight," he said. "It needs to be loosened up."

Remember, this was Jordan's first experience playing at the United Center. He had made his fame at the Chicago Stadium which had been across the street before it was removed to make way for the new stadium's parking lot. Jordan's poor shooting performances in the first few games back were obviously partially caused by his inactivity for 18 months, but he had certainly become accustomed to the soft landing spots the Stadium rims provided.

Jordan said he had no problems with the east rim at the UC, but the west rim was not to his liking. So he said he was taking hundreds of shots at the rim every chance he got, and hanging his strong body off the rim in an attempt to make it the way he liked it.

The story I wrote off the exchange became a key point for sportswriters the rest of the season, and well into the next couple of years as Jordan got familiar with the building that became known as "The House That Michael Built."

Jordan returned to normal in terms of his accessibility when the 1995–96 season started, although he was never as jovial as he had been before the first retirement.

33. Jordan Makes a Joke

Michael Jordan was not a funny person. He liked to laugh and he liked a practical joke. He enjoyed making fun of others, mostly good-naturedly, although he could be very biting when discussing a player's basketball ability. He had a great sense of humor, but he did not tell jokes.

Which made his setup and punch line in the Miami locker room that night all the more remarkable. He actually nailed the joke.

When the NBA opened up teams in Miami and Orlando, the Bulls got a new source of mid-winter sunlight. They also got Hooter's.

The restaurant, which features chicken wings and gorgeous, scantily clad waitresses, was a revelation to the Bulls, and Jordan was among them. He loved the place; the restaurant was a very short walk from the Coconut Grove hotel in which the team stayed when it played the Heat, and Jordan was there for lunch and postgame dinner whenever the Bulls were in south Florida.

The first time we were there, we had a very public appearance at Hooters. It was the day before the game; we had an extra day in town. I was there having lunch, and I actually think I saw every member of the team show up at some point that day. The waitresses were very friendly, and Jordan was not unfriendly back.

Before every road game, the visiting team gets its allotment of tickets to hand out to friends or family who happen to be in town. The more veteran the player, the more tickets he gets from the home team. Much of pregame is spent exchanging tickets. The players sign the envelopes the tickets are in, the envelopes are taken up to the will-call window, and the players' friends and acquaintances get to see the game.

And yes, players would sometimes give out tickets to women they just met or already knew. As conversation starters, it was a good and successful ploy.

I was in the locker room before the first game we played at Miami Arena and the players were divvying up their tickets. Jordan suddenly spoke up loudly.

"NO TICKETS FOR HOOTERS GIRLS," Jordan said, and there was a little bit of laughter.

Then Jordan said, "And I need 16 tickets."

He completely sold the setup and nailed the punch line. It may have been one of the funniest things he ever said.

34. Staying Alive in Miami

Going to Miami was fun; we stayed in Coconut Grove, which was party central. The team hotel, in which I usually stayed, was unique to the point of being weird, but it had a hot tub on the patio for every room. The league was always kind about giving us an extra day to play around in Miami before we were forced back to the real winter world of Chicago.

I took advantage. I had great meals, many late-night drinks, which were followed by many barely made early-morning flights.

One year, veteran NBA writer Sam Smith was on the trip, and I had my tennis racquets with me, and he and I found some courts near the hotel and played. It turned out, however, that we were about a block away from a very troubled area of the city, and that stained our enjoyment of the day.

Miami in the 1990s had many troubled areas, and one of them was around the stadium. At one point in the decade, there were some very serious, nationally televised riots in the Bucktown neighborhood, which surrounded the stadium.

That year, for the only time in all of my travels with the team, the referees for the game traveled with the team to the game for safety reasons. I was on the bus as well; the league wanted all personnel representing the league in some way to get safely to the game.

It was an unusual site to see the referees (I remember that veteran ref Dick Bavetta was one of them) get on the team bus to head for the stadium. Our approach to the game was quieter than usual.

Unfortunately, the team left after the game without us. That was as it always was; the reporters in attendance had to file stories, while the team would return to the hotel. They took the referees home, but we beat writers were left to fend for ourselves.

But we were from Chicago, and we were not afraid (a similar sentiment that almost froze us to death in Minneapolis one night). We told the media relations member who was in charge of the press room that we would just hail a cab.

"No, you won't," the media staffer said quietly. "There won't be any cabs outside."

The team had a security officer drive us back to our hotel, and we paid him the money we would have given the cabbie.

The second trip to Miami that season came at a time when the riots had settled, but the area had not improved. The *Tribune* sent Paul Sullivan, a veteran baseball writer, to cover the game in place of their regular writer, who was taking some time off. Sullivan had rented a car, and asked me to help him get to the stadium.

We arrived in the middle of the day, and it was not the least bit frightening.

After the game, we told the media relations staffer we had a car and were driving back to our hotel. The Heat representative made sure we had very clear directions, so that we had no trouble getting back.

And we had trouble. We missed a turn that was supposed to put us on a freeway, and instead we ended up exactly where the Heat staffer did not want us to end up. Sullivan drove with all possible purpose to get us to something that resembled safety.

I was also escorted to my car in Oakland while covering the Golden State Warriors, and locked in an outdoor parking lot in East Rutherford, New Jersey, while covering the Nets. But Miami was the scariest place I can remember.

There was a night when we beat writers put ourselves in danger, but it was only because of hubris that comes with being from Chicago.

We were covering a game in Minneapolis, at the Target Center, which was exactly three blocks from the City Center Marriott, where we all were staying. It was ridiculously cold outside; sub-zero temperature with a strong wind blowing in from the west. In Minneapolis, I guess, that is known as "Thursday."

I walked to the game with *Tribune* beat writer Terry Armour and *Sun-Times* beat writer John Jackson, and we hustled. When the game was over, a media relations representative offered to give us a ride to the hotel.

I know Minneapolis weather is severe, but we were from Chicago. We had to represent. So we said, "No thank you" and began our leisurely walk to the Marriott.

It was 11:00 PM. Our walk required us to leave the stadium from the north side, walk half a block, then through an open-air parking lot that took up an entire city block. Then we had another short block to get to the hotel.

We realized before we got to the parking lot that we had made a big mistake. It was the kind of cold that you hope you live through so you can tell somebody about it someday. The parking lot looked like it was half a mile wide. We could turn back, but the door locked behind us and we didn't want to take the chance that no one would hear us scream.

So we started to run. Of the three of us, I was in the best shape; Armour and Jackson were not that well-conditioned. But they moved when they needed to.

Screaming to each other with the scream of the desperate, we agreed that if the side door to the hotel was not open, we were dead. Thankfully, the side door opened (had this happened post 9/11, it would have been over for us) and we survived.

35. Dennis Rodman

It was October 1995. Michael Jordan was back from his first retirement and was going to play another full season for the Bulls after the embarrassment in the playoff series against Orlando the season before, when he came back from retirement and was not physically ready to play at the highest level.

The Bulls still had all of the players general manager Jerry Krause had claimed in order to prepare the team to continue its championship run after the third title in 1993. Krause had plans to recreate the Bulls around a new set of veterans who could play with Jordan and Scottie

Pippen, and all of those players were ready to go to work for the start of the 1995–96 season.

Then came the news that Krause had pulled off a major coup, a trade of epic proportions, as he sent backup center Will Perdue to the San Antonio Spurs for troubled and troubling power forward Dennis Rodman, known (disaffectionately in Chicago) as "The Worm." In the world of the Chicago Bulls, no player could have been added to the roster that would have been more potentially problematic; no headline would have been bigger.

This was the Rodman who had been on the Bad Boys of Detroit, who had twisted and turned his way through numerous games against the Bulls, both when the Pistons ruled the league and when the Bulls finally surpassed them. This was the Dennis Rodman who had pushed Scottie Pippen into a basketball stanchion, resulting in a scar that Pippen still has to this day.

This was the Dennis Rodman who could not stay on the court in San Antonio because of behavioral problems. And yet, that first week of October 1995, I was attending a press conference to introduce Rodman to the Chicago fans and media.

In professional sports, you rarely experience moments that are actually surreal. Seeing Dennis Rodman at the press conference that day to play for the Bulls was a surreal experience.

The Bulls prided themselves on having players of good character. It wasn't just talk; during the Krause years, there were very few incidents of criminal activity or poor choices. In this case, the Bulls actually did have a roster full of good guys.

Rodman was a lot of things to a lot of people. No one was going to hold him up as a role model.

Most people remember what he looked like that day as the Bulls presented him to the media at the Berto Center. He had the Bulls logo laid out in black in his nappy hair, which was blood red. He had all of those facial rings—in lips and eyebrows and nose. He was a sight, a new sight to Chicago.

At his introductory press conference, Rodman explained what the Bulls were looking at going forward with The Worm as their starting power forward.

"They won't have any problem with Dennis Rodman as long as they can handle what Dennis Rodman can put on the basketball floor and off the court," he said.

"Off the court?" Nobody could handle what Rodman had to offer off the court. Even the David Robinson–led Spurs, in a small market where one really had to go searching for trouble, could not handle Rodman off the court.

The Bulls were operating from a position of strength. No team and no organization was respected more in the NBA at the time. If there was a team that could convert Rodman into a solid citizen on and off the court, it was the Bulls.

"Phil [Jackson] and I have complete confidence this is going to work out extremely well," Bulls general manager Jerry Krause said. I swear I heard someone whistling in the wind as he said those words.

At the end of the press conference, with the final question, I asked Rodman how he was doing from a personal standpoint. His two-year stint with the Spurs, which followed his lengthy and very successful time with the Detroit Pistons, had been marred by on-the-court and off-the-court incidents, which is why the Spurs were so happy to take center Will Perdue in exchange for the spectacular Rodman.

"I'm doing great," he said. "I think I'm fitting into the world and society very well."

If that is not a sentence that screams, "It hasn't always been that way," I don't know one that does.

A couple of days later, we beat writers got some alone time with Jordan to discuss how he was going to handle what Rodman had to offer.

"I am not going to take that responsibility because there are other players who have feelings for this team," he said. "If anything happens and we have to [talk to Rodman] we will do it as a team. Whatever Dennis does, I think we will talk to him collectively.

"I think everybody is condemning this man before he even steps on the court," he said. "I believe in giving the guy an opportunity to prove himself. Maybe he is a changed guy. Maybe he understands things better than you think he does."

As it turned out, Jordan was correct. Rodman did understand things better than one might expect. He didn't always handle things well, but he knew the parameters in front of him.

I was completely uninterested in covering Dennis Rodman. I knew him from his days as a Piston. He was brash and mean and sullen and uncooperative and in some ways a dirty player. He had attempted to injure Scottie Pippen in a game by throwing him into the stanchion under the basket in a game.

I did not want to have to cover the circus that was sure to follow him.

But it turned out much better than expected. I found Rodman to be thoughtful, engaging, far more intelligent than I would have guessed, introspective, and willing to talk. In small groups, or even those occasions when I had him alone, I could not have asked for a better conversational partner.

When he got in front of the bright lights, he became someone else, someone I did not like.

Rodman would rarely hold still for a large group interview with reporters. He made us walk with him as he exited one building or another. It was demeaning. Among reporters, it became known as the Walk of Shame. I would not do it, not after the first couple of times when I got nothing meaningful out of the experience.

But I amaze everyone when his name comes up, because I honestly enjoyed his company. Who would have guessed?

In one of the first preseason games that season, a game played at home, a play developed in which Jordan found himself guarded by a much smaller player, and he called for the ball from Rodman, who was holding the ball near the top of the key. Rodman waved Jordan to go into the post, and as Jordan put his back to the basket with the smaller defender on him, Rodman gave him the pass that led to an easy turn-around jumper for a basket.

After the game, at the usual Jordan gang-bang where I rarely asked questions, I said, "Michael, in the third quarter there was that play where Dennis waved you into the post then passed you the ball for an easy basket. How did it feel seeing Dennis Rodman setting you up like that?"

Jordan smiled one of those truly genuine smiles that he sometimes got when he was asked to come out of the shell of standard cliché answers for the media. "Yeah, it was definitely weird," he said.

And that was just the beginning.

36. Michael Jordan's Wallet

In the early years of my relationship with Jordan, I found him to be about as normal as a widely popular and famous and respected person could be. He liked to kid around, he loved to make good-natured fun of people, and he loved to laugh.

By the time I got to know him, he had gotten out of the jewelry phase of his life (do you remember the necklace he wore the first time he was in the Slam-Dunk competition?) and he never let it be known in locker room conversation that he was better off financially than anybody else in the room. He was interested (or feigned interest) whenever the conversation turned to the mundane lives of the reporters in the room.

Only once in my time with him did he "hit me with his wallet." We were sitting next to each other in the locker room and he was looking at a catalogue of high-end cars. I have never ever been a car guy, looking at my automobiles as just a way to get from one place to another. But this time it was my turn to feign interest as he pointed to a car he was thinking of buying.

"What do you think?" he asked me.

"Out of my price range," I told him.

"It's not out of mine."

That was the only time money ever came up with Jordan as a way to compare one's worth.

37. Autographs

I have never been asked for my autograph, except for those times when someone thought I was someone else.

When I was covering sports in Indianapolis for United Press International, I covered the U.S. Open Clay Court Tennis Championships. I was a tennis player myself, and during the tournament they always held a media tournament prior to the event.

The tournament was held in August, and it can get quite warm in Indianapolis in August. I often dressed accordingly even when I was covering the event, and sometimes wore the same outfit I would wear if I was going to play tennis.

The interview area was below the stands at the tennis facility, so I would use the same stairs to exit as the players. One day, I was walking up the stairs and got to the main concourse. I had my media badge on, but it was not much different than the badges the players wore to identify themselves. A child of about nine years old was at the top of the stairs with a program from the event, and she asked me very politely if I would sign it. She thought I was a player.

As a lark, I did. (I looked around first, though, to make sure no one in authority saw me doing it). The funny part was, as I looked up from signing the one program, I was surrounded by about six other kids wanting me to sign their book. I signed a couple more and then headed for the hills.

I tell that story because there were at least two times I signed my name to an item because a fan thought I was someone important with the Bulls. I have to assume they thought I was a player, although I was (and am) only 5'9". And I wear glasses. And I don't look like a basketball player in any way.

I remember it happened once in Atlanta as we were all waiting for our bags to show up in luggage claim. A youngster had a notebook and got everybody on the team to sign it, including me. Imagine, a piece of paper with both my signature and Michael's on it. That's got to be worth a pretty penny.

On the back of the official NBA press pass, it says reporters are not allowed to ask players for autographs. It would never have occurred to me to do so. And I never did. I covered Jordan for 14 years, 11 as a beat writer, and never once got his autograph on anything. Except a bowling pin.

38. Luc Longley

Weird how many things I remember happened at the Los Angeles Sports Arena.

I didn't much like the place. It was old, and compared to the Great Western Forum where the Lakers played, it was far behind the times. It was befitting the Clippers, who were L.A.'s bastard son of a franchise.

One time on the way to the Coliseum, I got a little lost and ended up driving through Watts. This was in the 1990s, 30 years after the famous riots, but it was still Watts. I was going to be extra careful.

But I wasn't careful enough. I stopped at a stop sign and got bumped by the car behind me. I looked in my rear-view mirror and saw a mom with two kids hopping around in the car. The contact was slight, and I sure wasn't going to get out right there to inspect the damage. I would let my insurance company handle it if it came to that.

I raised my hand to the woman, and she waved back, seeming to indicate she was okay. And that's all I needed. I drove off and found my way to the Coliseum.

I was going to shootaround practice at the Coliseum one day in 1997, and there I found Luc Longley with his shoulder bandaged. He had not been hurt in any game, so I asked him what was up.

Turns out, during our off-day the day before, he and Jud Buechler had gone out to hit the waves. Longley is from Australia (the first

Michael Jordan, Luc Longley, and Steve Kerr watch from the bench as their teammates play Olympiakos during the McDonald's Championship at the Palais Omnisports De Paris-Bercy in Paris, France. *(Photo courtesy Getty Images)*

Australian to play in the NBA) and we all know how famous Australia is for the waves. Buechler was raised in Southern California, so hitting the waves was in his blood, too.

The two were body surfing. Now, you might think there would be some sort of codicil in the contract of professional athletes that they won't do anything stupid with their bodies on the off-days, but that was not the case. In fact, Bulls coach Phil Jackson liked to have the players lead lives of some normalcy as well as excitement in their off-days.

Still, the Bulls were without their starting center as a result of what happened. Longley was heading into the beach on a wave, but he slammed his shoulder into a hidden sandbar near the beach and separated it.

Although he had been treated by the team trainer, when I saw him he had not yet told Jackson what happened, and he did not want to.

"What do you think he will say?" Longley asked me.

"He will probably ask you about the surf," I told him.

Longley was not amused.

Jackson actually handled the incident well. He had always encouraged players to experience life outside of basketball, and admitted the team was paying a price for that philosophy with the temporary loss of Longley. But it did not change his attitude toward extracurricular activities.

Of all of the players on the second three-peat teams, I was closest to Pippen, but I really enjoyed both Longley and Toni Kukoc. Maybe it was because they were foreigners. In Longley's case, it was pretty difficult not to like him. He was known as the Affable Aussie, a name he picked up when he played in Minnesota before he joined the Bulls, and the nickname was apropos.

Longley taught all of his teammates and reporters to say both "G'day" and "No Worries." I really think he lived his life with a "no worries" point of view. When Jackson would berate him for poor play (Longley just wasn't as physical and imposing as he should have been at 7'2"), he would look at his coach with a hidden bemusement. He knew, in the grander scheme of things, that it just didn't matter. Not that he did not try to be the best player he could be, he could just live with his limitations.

I do remember one serious conversation we had. His wife was pregnant with his second daughter, and he told me his wife was going to deliver the baby at home under the watchful eye of a midwife, which is how they do things back home. He asked me to keep that part quiet, and I was quietly pleased he felt secure enough in our relationship that he could tell me and ask me to keep it between us.

One year, we were in Orlando, and we had a night off. Jimmy Buffett, the famed singer who wrote "Margaritaville" was performing at the Orlando Arena. Paxson and I had seen him on numerous occasions and went to see him again, this time with Longley, Bill Wennington, and Steve Kerr.

We were staying at the Orlando Marriott, which was just across the parking lot from the Arena, so we walked over. I was exactly 17 inches shorter than Longley, and my stride was significantly shorter. For some reason, I had trouble keeping up, and Longley looked back at me at one point and said, "C'mon, little buddy."

We met Buffett before the show, then we got into our seats, and that night I had to be the most popular attendee for the people sitting behind me, because I sat between Longley and Wennington, another 7-footer. Everybody wanted to sit behind me.

39. The National Anthem

Before every sporting event from high school on, there is some sort of rendition of the national anthem presented. In high school and college, it is often a recording, unless it is football, when the band does the duties. In professional sports, it is usually sung by a professional singer, or performed by a musician while the audience either listens or, on occasion, sings along.

It always seemed like a silly sort of tradition to me. I'm as proud of being an American as the next guy, but one does not prove his devotion by singing a song (or by not singing it). Often, the audience would not participate, and it was just a quiet arena listening to a recording for about 90 seconds.

Besides, the song itself is impossible to sing well, and the lyrics made no sense in the 20th century.

Listening to some really sad renditions of the national anthem was a part of the price I paid for the opportunity to cover sports for a living. A price I paid willingly, until that day in New Jersey, January 21, 1993.

The New Jersey Nets played basketball in East Rutherford, New Jersey, a community north of Newark, and when I was covering the Bulls, the Nets were a difficult draw. They were never a good team, and they had to go to extremes to get fans to come to the middle of nowhere for games. The stadium seemed out of the way. Even though they were at one time the New York Nets, they did not draw from the New York population particularly well.

Which is why they asked Olympic track star and entertainer-wannabe Carl Lewis to sing the national anthem. Lewis, like so many Olympic athletes, was trying to find a place for himself in the entertainment world after his athletic career was over, and he decided he was going to be a recording artist.

So Lewis took center court before the game, the public address announcer told everyone that Olympic gold medal sprinter Carl Lewis was about to sing the Star-Spangled Banner, and there was a sense of excitement, because Carl Lewis was a handsome superstar athlete. They love celebrity in the Tri-State area. And who knew Carl Lewis could sing?

But what happened about a minute later defied all tradition and defiled the national anthem. Lewis started off with a wail of some sort to set the tone, I guess, and really wanted to sing his heart out to show that he had the style and chops to make a second career out of performing.

But, as often happens, the song got the better of him. He completely messed up the lyrics about one-third of the way through, and then, to compound his mistake, he just stopped singing mid-song.

At one point, Lewis said, "Uh-oh" after one mistake. As he began the last stanza, he said, "I'll make up for it now."

There is YouTube video of excerpts of the performance, followed by two ESPN anchors laughing tremendously hard at what they had just heard. If you want to see why I was permanently affected by the performance, take a look and listen.

Johnny Bach, one of the Bulls' assistant coaches, was not laughing at Lewis' failed attempt. Bach is a proud former Marine. He never took kindly to players playing games with their shirts untucked, disrespecting their status as players in the premier basketball league in the world. He certainly didn't tolerate any disrespect shown to the United States of America. He hated any rendition of the national anthem that took liberties with the cadence of the song, any stylized attempt to make it the singer's song, rather than the nation's song.

When it was time for the national anthem, Bach would not watch the players, some who paid attention to the song, but many who closed their eyes and tolerated the 90 seconds or two minutes the song took. Bach would stand ramrod straight, at attention, from the start to the end, eyes focused squarely on the American flag, wherever it might be hanging.

After my own initial pained reaction to Lewis' performance, I looked over at Bach, who was to my left, standing in front of the Bulls' bench. I had seen Bach cringe at other odd attempts to sing the song. But when Lewis offered his apology, and as he started singing the song again, I didn't know whether Bach was going to cry or take to the floor, commandeer the microphone, and sing the song himself.

That was the last time I willingly stood in the basketball area for the national anthem of any game I covered. Lewis' performance was not the first time I had heard someone mess up the words to the song.

But his was the worst, and I just could not stand to put myself through that pain again. I couldn't stand it, and I wasn't going to stand it if I didn't have to. So, when I knew it was nearing time for the national anthem before any Bulls game, I would high-tail it to the back hallways of the arena, back where the locker rooms or press room were, until the song was over. Sometimes the performance was piped into the area where I was, and I would have to find some way to divert my attention so I did not concentrate on the song. Even with that precaution, I heard some terrible renditions and I could not ignore the times the singer got the words wrong.

Everybody I worked with covering the Bulls knew that was my tradition. Many years later, one of my colleagues, John Jackson of the *Chicago Sun-Times*, saw me talking to someone else at press row just seconds before the anthem started and yelled out, "Kent! National anthem!" and I actually ran out of the basketball bowl to find a quiet spot.

If I knew the song was being performed by a non-singing musician, I would stay and listen. One time, when the Bulls were playing the Indiana Pacers in Indianapolis, the national anthem was performed by a group of students from the Indiana School for the Deaf, who signed the lyrics with their hands while the words were displayed on the stadium's giant video screen above the center of the floor. It was a moving performance, the audience sang the song to match the signing, and that rendition goes down as my favorite.

I also have to tell you about one of my favorite moments when I was trapped and had to listen to the national anthem. I was covering a college basketball game, and had no place to go. I had to stand at press row while the song was performed by a college student.

But what happened before the performance is what made the moment special. Someone important had died the week prior to the game, and the public address announcer said, "Everyone please rise, remove your hats and observe a moment of silence" for the significant person.

After the minute passed, the P.A. announcer said, "Now, please continue to rise for the national anthem."

I laughed then (I still laugh when I tell the story). I tried, I really did, to "continue to rise." But I didn't have it in me. I stayed at the same height, and hoped no one would notice that I failed in my attempt.

40. Toni Kukoc

Inever got to see Toni Kukoc play for his team in Italy, but I knew just how famous and respected he was over there. His appearance in the United States, after years of cajoling from the Bulls, was dramatic for him.

He came over in the summer of 1993 to play with Michael Jordan, only to have Jordan retire days after he arrived. I will never forget seeing Kukoc well up with tears at the press conference when Jordan announced his decision. I can just imagine what he must have thought, leaving the comfort of Italy for the rigors of the NBA, joining a team that had two of the top players in the world in Jordan and Pippen, who also happened to have reason to hate him because of the attention he got from general manager Jerry Krause.

But I give Kukoc so much credit for the way he handled things. He rarely got angry at what was happening to him. What he did was implore people to treat him fairly.

He was really used by the officials. Why they would have it out for him, I don't know, but he needed a couple of seasons in the league before the referees would give him a fair shake. One game in San Antonio, he had a very bad night with the whistle blowers.

"Let's wait until next year and see what happens, if there is some change," Kukoc told me. "Against Dallas, I was once trying to say, 'Foul' and the ref said, 'No way.' In San Antonio, I looked at the ref once and he asked, 'What do you want?'"

That first year in the NBA, 1993–94, Kukoc had a chance to speak with former Yugoslavian teammate Vlade Divac, who played for the Los Angeles Lakers. Their friendship had been strained by the war between the Serbian and Croatian peoples, and that war had broken up one of the best basketball teams in the history of international play, with Divac, Kukoc, Drazen Petrovic and others.

The two players said hello before the game, then met again at the scorer's table as they prepared to enter the game in the second half.

"I had not talked to him in about three years," Kukoc said.

41. The Ron Harper Story

When Ron Harper came to the Bulls in 1994, he had already been in the league for eight seasons, and they had not gone the way he would have liked. He left the University of Miami (Ohio) to join his hometown team, the Cleveland Cavaliers, as the eighth overall pick in the draft, but he could not lead them to a level of significance. He played just three seasons for the Cavs before being traded to the Los Angeles Clippers, where he spent five seasons. His time in L.A. was negatively affected by a knee injury that hampered his playing ability.

He was supposed to be the poor man's Michael Jordan, but did not have Jordan's competitive nature or stature. But when he came to the Bulls, he was to be the veteran backcourt sidekick to Jordan, splitting time with Jordan as the point guard or shooting guard, depending on who had the ball in their hands.

Scottie Pippen, Ron Harper, and Toni Kukoc celebrate after defeating the SuperSonics for the Bulls fourth title of the dynasty.

Harper also suffered from a severe stutter that made him a difficult interview at times if you didn't have patience to wait him out.

But he was a kindhearted man, and he was also a twin. That's why he took special interest when I was about to add twins to my family.

My wife was due in early June of 1996, and we wondered if the twins were going to come on the birthday of our older child Haley, who was born on June 1. But the twins did not come until June 5, which happened to be the first game of the Bulls-Seattle NBA finals. So I missed the first game of the series to be with my wife.

Dan and Lindsey were born two minutes apart, and my wife was induced into labor because Lindsey was not growing properly (Dan was eating her food, doctors told us). When she arrived, she was only four pounds, two ounces, and because babies lose weight almost immediately after being born, Lindsey had to stay in the hospital for five days after her birth in order to gain weight.

I went back to work on June 7 for the second game of the series in Chicago, and then went to Seattle for the week of games from June 9 to 14, flying home during that time to spend time with Janice and Dan and to help Lindsey come home.

I had told Harper and the other players that my daughter was in the hospital and I was concerned about her, and Harper always asked a lot of questions. He was also dismayed that we had named the kids as we did, because he was of the opinion twins had to have rhyming names like he and his brother Don.

On June 16, 1996, the Bulls beat the Sonics in Game 6 of the series to claim their fourth title in six years and the first of the second three-peat. Harper had been a key contributor to that title as the starting guard, and the championship was the successful culmination of a career that had spanned 10 years at that point.

When the game was over and the Bulls were celebrating in the locker room at the relatively new United Center, I had to talk to every member of the team that mattered, including Harper. I had not spoken to him that day until after the game, and he was enjoying his champagne like everyone else. But when I approached him, I shook his hand and said congratulations, and he said, "How's Lindsey?"

Just minutes after winning the biggest title of his career in the game he had played his entire life, he had the nature to ask me about my daughter, who had had a pretty rough first 10 days of her life. That's perspective right there.

42

Home Indeed Proves To Be Sweet
June 17, 1996

Those 72 wins apparently did mean something after all.

Breaking the league record for wins in a season allowed the Bulls to have homecourt advantage through every round of the playoffs. Returning home after a disappointing week in Seattle, the Bulls on Sunday recorded their 10th playoff win at home, their 15th win of the postseason, their 87th win of the 1995–96 season, and their fourth championship of the decade.

Now, it is up to history to decide the significance of the 1995–96 Bulls, who entered the playoffs with the best record in league history and the battle cry, "It don't mean a thing without the ring."

"This has been a very, very special year for me," said Michael Jordan, who scored 22 points and earned his fourth NBA Finals Most Valuable Player award. "No way you could really describe it."

The Bulls, who beat the Super Sonics 87–75 to win the final series 4–2, ended the campaign as the league's winningest, oddest, and most talked about team ever. Jordan's return to finest form, the revival of Scottie Pippen's role as the league's second-best player, and the unfathomable addition of the once-hated Dennis Rodman produced a team capable of winning any game it played.

After submitting for league approval an unprecedented regular-season record of 72–10, the Bulls cruised to the edge of history, winning 14 of their first 15 playoff games before failing twice in Seattle last week. But they returned home, took control of the game in the first quarter, and built momentum on the way to the victory.

"It was very special," said Pippen, who had one of his better games of the series with 17 points, eight rebounds, five assists, and four steals. "I felt we had done something no other team had done. To bring this team together in one season, this is very special because I think we all as players and as individuals had a lot we wanted to prove. We wanted to show the world we were the greatest team."

What they proved is they were the best team in the NBA this season. History will wait awhile before deciding where to place the Bulls on the roster of great basketball teams.

Sunday, the Bulls were certainly a team. With Jordan making only 5-of-19 shots from the field, Dennis Rodman provided 19 rebounds—11 off the offensive glass—center Luc Longley made 5-of-6 shots and pulled down eight rebounds, and Ron Harper returned from a four-day hiatus due to knee pain to score 10 points in 38 minutes.

"I knew I could play today," Harper said. "I got to rest M.J. some. I got to rest all week."

The bench contributed as well. Toni Kukoc, the European import, returned to his bench role to score 10 points with two key three-pointers, and Steve Kerr broke out of his slump to make 3-of-4 shots for seven points.

For the Sonics, who pushed the Bulls further than any team all season, Shawn Kemp maintained his role as the team MVP, scoring 18 points with 14 rebounds. Gary Payton had

19 points, but the Sonics were out-rebounded 51–35 and out-scored from the free-throw line 16–8.

"We just couldn't ever play well on this court," said Seattle coach George Karl. "I think Chicago is a team we were getting closer to every game, and we were gaining confidence every game."

Jordan was 1-of-5 from the field in the first quarter, an indication of the kind of shooting night he would have. But the Bulls did not need Jordan to be brilliant Sunday.

The Bulls had a 45–38 halftime lead, and Seattle's Gary Payton made a three-pointer to start the second half, cutting the difference to four points. But Harper answered with his own three-pointer, and when he made his second bomb of the quarter the Bulls were ahead 55–45. Seattle got no closer than nine points the rest of the game, in part because Rodman would not let any loose ball get away. He had seven of his rebounds in the fourth quarter.

"Dennis did everything to help us win," Longley said. "Without him, there is no doubt we wouldn't have won."

When the game was over, the Bulls stayed on the floor with the exception of Jordan, who went into the locker room to have a private moment with his feelings, remembering his slain father, James. When he returned to the floor, the picture was complete, and the season was over.

"The pleasant surprise was the way we jelled together," Jordan said. "There was no animosity, no bickering. There was no jealousy. We were able to maintain a certain focus and we have accomplished history."

43. Pippen Calls His Shot

The comparison between Jordan and Pippen was ongoing and never-ending. Pippen could never win. Despite a larger wingspan and similar physical abilities, Pippen was rarely ever considered "better" than Jordan at anything.

But Pippen was a better defender than Jordan. He did a better job of facing up to an opponent with the ball. Jordan was fond of the wrap-around strip if a player got by him. Pippen never had to rely on that.

Offensively, Pippen was not as stylish with his dunks. He almost never dribbled between his legs the way Jordan would when he was sizing up a defender.

But one thing Pippen was better at than Jordan offensively was making bank shots.

By the time Jordan came back from his first retirement to recreate magic, Pippen was the best bank-shot shooter in the league. He was deadly. He knew the spots on the backboard the way every school boy basketball player in the United States does. He almost reintroduced the bank shot in the NBA.

I was a bank shooter when I played. I think I liked the geometry and physics involved. So when I saw Pippen develop the shot, I talked to him about it.

"There was a time when I felt more comfortable driving [to the basket], but now I feel comfortable just shooting the ball if my legs are in the right position and it is the right time of the game," Pippen said. "I try to just play now and not really think about the shots that I am taking. I'm just taking what the defense gives me."

44. Jackson

I was thrilled to get to know Phil Jackson initially.

My relationship with coach Doug Collins was strained because I really don't think he ever tried to tell the truth about things. He avoided controversial remarks and whitewashed so many things, perhaps in an attempt to appease his bosses. Since he left the Bulls, he's had a few other coaching jobs, and it seems like he's opened up a bit more. He also worked with the national media in between coaching gigs, and that made him a bit more responsive to the needs of reporters.

I expected Jackson to be more forthcoming. His hippie background and his non-establishment attitude would hopefully manifest itself when he took over as coach in 1989.

My first real conversation with Jackson occurred when he was an assistant. We were at the lobby bar at the Westin Hotel in Boston after a game, and he talked about books, a favorite topic of mine. He told me what he was reading, I told him what I was reading, and we began our relationship.

That continued when he was the head coach. I was already on the bus re-reading my favorite book of all time, and he was quick to remark.

"Atlas Shrugged?" he said with surprise. "That's a serious book. Have you read [Ayn Rand's] other books?

Another time I was reading Don Quixote on the bus, and Jackson was really excited. He told me to get back to him when I was done with the book, because he had a point he wanted to make. I don't think that conversation ever took place.

Jackson would often work the *New York Times* crossword puzzle in the locker room before a game, and I was always pleased on those rare occasions when I was able to supply him with an answer he did not

Phil Jackson shows off the NBA Coach of the Year trophy that he was awarded after leading the Bulls to a 72–10 record.

know. Often it was pop culture related, so I don't think I scored any genius points, but it pleased me.

Jackson and I played tennis together once. We were in Phoenix at the Ritz-Carlton, which had very nice tennis courts. We were on a long road trip west so I had my racquets, and Jackson knew I was playing against Craig Hodges during the trip, so he said he would play.

It was unusual, because Jackson is 6'8". He could not really run, but he often did not have to. His height made me alter my game. I started hitting nothing but shots that forced him to bend. He also couldn't bend. But he had a great shot, and considering he probably had not played tennis in a long while, he did well.

(You might be wondering if any of these contacts with athletes and coaches away from the job benefitted me on the job. The answer is yes, but not in the way you might think. I think it made me appear as a normal Joe, not one of the evil empire out to "get" athletes in one way or another, either by word or by deed. I also know it never affected my decision on writing a negative story. My inherent objectivity was fairly apparent to everyone I worked with. They knew I had no agenda.)

I appreciated the fact that Jackson was a thinking man's coach. I never did well with jughead athletes or coaches, the guys who could not speak of anything outside the lines, or if they did, it was whatever the opposite of intellectual is.

My favorite coaching ploy of Jackson's, one that I noticed right away, was that he was very strategic about his timeouts, and most of strategy had to do with not using them. If the opponent was going on an offensive run and the Bulls were struggling to match the effort and result, Jackson would let them play through it. It was his philosophy that the team had to figure out on its own what to do in that situation, just in case there was a time when timeouts were at a premium.

Jackson often seemed to look forward to my questions. I often waited out most press conferences because others would ask the questions I wanted answers to, and many times reporters wanted to get noticed, to get some recognition from players and coaches.

Also, as I said before, I tried to ask questions that had never been asked prior to my involvement in the game.

The best example I can remember is when I noticed that the Bulls were one of the top-ranked teams in the league in the never-before-examined statistic of free throw defense. The league puts out all sorts of statistics on the game, and they include not only a team's free throw percentage, but also their opponents' free throw percentage, as if that is an area a team can work on in order to win a couple more games.

That sort of stuff cracks me up, so I had a secret smile on my face when we were on the road somewhere, getting quotes from a practice in between games, and I asked Jackson about the team's impressive free throw defense statistics.

"It's all of our harassment," Jackson said with a smile.

45. He Went To Paris

Nobody wants to know that being a sportswriter can sometimes stink.

For many young men and women, being a sportswriter is a dream job. You get paid to attend sporting events! You get to talk to the players! You get in the locker room! You know all the inside stuff.

Fans do not want to know that the job is an all-day job (which is especially true today with social media requiring near constant attention). They don't want to know that players often, very often, disregard the media. They don't want to know that players and coaches see reporters as a nuisance. They don't want to know that editors want access that reporters can't possibly achieve. They don't want to know about the pressure of competition that exists between reporters on the same beat.

And fans sure do not want to hear how exhausting it is to travel as a beat writer in the NBA.

True NBA fans know that when a league requires 82 games be played in six months, which is about 180 days, that there are times teams must play three games in four nights. They know that such schedules can often include three days of travel. They know that all NBA teams end up in six- or seven-game road trips which cover nine or 10 days. They know all about how tired the players can be from such rigors.

But they don't want to know the same is true for the reporters who cover the team. And, while many of my colleagues moan about how tired they are after a Minneapolis-to-Toronto-to-Chicago three-day swing, they never heard such a cry from me.

I loved the traveling I did when I covered the NBA.

The American history to be found in Boston and Philadelphia, the weather in Miami and Orlando, the unusual culture in Los Angeles, the entirely different culture in San Francisco, the remarkable beauty of Seattle or Vancouver. Denver, Phoenix, Toronto, New Orleans—I went to all the great cities of North America and often got to spend an entire afternoon walking the downtown streets to study the architecture, sample the food, and meet the people.

You never heard me complain about the travel related to my job. Even the flight delays, the hotel mix-ups, the occasional bad meal or rushed meal—I knew I was living what for some was a dream and I was not going to complain about the privilege.

I must credit the *Daily Herald*, which did not have the same budget as either the *Tribune* or the *Sun-Times* but which never complained to me about the money they were spending to help me help them with coverage of the most famous sports beat in the nation at the time. I did what I could to save money by getting the best hotel rates and taking the cheapest flights, but I was not pressured to do any of those things.

When it was announced that the Bulls were going to be playing in the McDonald's Championship in Paris in the early fall of 1997, I knew there was little chance I would get to go. It would be a loss for the paper, because the *Tribune* and *Sun-Times* were going to be sending multiple people to watch the Bulls play Europe's best club teams in an exhibition series.

I was going to be fine with the decision not to go. I was disappointed, but not dejected.

My international traveling at that point consisted of a pair of trips to the United Kingdom, plus visits to Canada and Mexico. It is a lifelong regret that I never had the chance, or took the opportunity, to explore more of the world. Certainly, if I had been asked where in the world I would like to go that I had not yet visited, Paris was not high on the list. I much preferred the idea of someday seeing Austria or the Scandinavian countries or Spain and Italy before Paris and France.

The *Herald* was not always quick to make a big decision. So I was not entirely surprised when, 10 days before the first game in Paris, they decided I should indeed go to cover the games.

Holy crap! Ten days to prepare for a trip to Paris. I suddenly needed an updated passport, plane tickets, and permission from my wife. I had to make preparations for dealing with our three kids, who were all pre-kindergarten age. I was suddenly in the rush of my life.

I also wanted to brush up on my French. I took six years of the language in middle school and high school and I was not going to be an ugly American, trying to make everyone speak English to me. I knew the French almost all spoke English anyway, but I also knew that they appreciated when visitors at least tried to speak their language, and I was going to do more than try. I was going to succeed.

Amazingly, I found a flight at a price that was not going to make the paper fold. I even had a great seat, a first row seat in the economy section that had tons of leg room in front of me.

I made my travel plans, which included not sleeping at all the night before, so I could sleep on the plane. I knew that I was going to have to run to cover a introductory press conference the moment I arrived, so I planned to get at least some sleep on the plane so I would be work-worthy upon landing.

That plan did not work. I did not sleep one wink. I tried a glass of wine, I tried everything, but I could not sleep. The effects of that unfortunate turn of events will be explained later.

The Bulls were going to play two games while in Paris, one against PSG Racing, the French club champion, and one against Olympiakos, the Greek club champion. There were three other teams invited: Benetton Treviso of Italy (Toni Kukoc's old team), FC Barcelona, and Athenas de Cordoba of Argentina. The Bulls were one of two teams getting a first-round bye in the six-team tournament.

The McDonald's Championship had been played every two years starting in 1987 between an NBA representative and several international basketball club teams, and the NBA teams had never lost a game. In 1995, while Jordan was enjoying his first retirement, the NBA champion Houston Rockets attended, the first time the league sent its champion, and that set the stage for the 1997 NBA Champion Bulls to do the same.

Other teams that had played in the tournament included the NBA teams from Milwaukee, Boston, Denver, New York, Los Angeles (Lakers), and Phoenix.

The Bulls did not have two of their top three players on the trip. Scottie Pippen did not make the trip because of summer foot surgery and Dennis Rodman was not there because he was recovering from a severe bout of pneumonia. Rodman also did not yet have a contract for the 1997–98 season, and there was some belief the team was holding off on signing him so he would not be with the team in Paris, thus avoiding an international incident of some sort.

The Bulls arrived in Paris on Tuesday afternoon and prepared for a game Friday night against PSG Racing.

I arrived in Paris in the late morning Wednesday and needed to get to a noon press conference downtown. John Jackson, my colleague from the *Sun-Times*, was on the same flight so we took a cab together from Charles de Gaulle Airport. I impressed Jackson with my conversation with the cabdriver, all in French, even though I was limited mostly to two- and three-word contributions.

Upon our arrival at the league hotel, I was told my hotel arrangements had been changed, but I could not immediately worry about that. I had to get to the press conference, which was with Jordan and Coach Jackson. Jordan, who had golfed on Tuesday afternoon after practice, said he planned to do a little sight-seeing with his family, who were on the trip with him. Jackson was asked if he would limit Jordan's minutes, even if a game was on the line.

"Not if it threatens winning," he said. "I think the NBA has something to uphold. It is a status we have to uphold."

After the press conference, I found out where my hotel was, and I dragged my bag across Paris to the new location, which was very nice. My room was dark, but I managed to get my computer running and I dealt with the change in electrical outlets as I had planned. Then I sat down to write.

And I fell asleep. Again and again, I fell asleep. I would wake up, type a couple of sentences, and fall asleep at the computer. I would wake up to see that in my sleep I had typed some gibberish. I had to delete the gobbledygook, figure out what I was trying to say before I fell asleep, then write some more. It took me forever to get the story done. When I did, I went to sleep like a normal person.

I got up in time to enjoy dinner Wednesday evening, and found out that the team had been invited to an NBA-sponsored dinner with all of the teams. The players and coaches mingled, and it was especially enjoyable for Kukoc, who was a European star for so many years before joining the Bulls. He admittedly had a great time, feeling at home perhaps for the first time since 1994.

"I pretty much knew everybody at the dinner," Kukoc told me.

The next day there was another press conference, this time including Dragan Tarlac, a Yugoslavian native who was well-known for his play with the Greek team in the tournament. The Bulls had drafted Tarlac in the 1995 NBA draft, hoping he would be the next Kukoc, but that day he expressed his hesitation about coming over to the U.S. (He eventually did so, and his hesitation proved to be warranted, as he had little success.)

On Thursday, after writing, I had the best time possible. I walked and walked and walked, and saw all of the sites one sees when one visits Paris. I could not get over the Eiffel Tower; I stood at its base and stared for many minutes. I went to the top of the Arc de Triumph. I walked the Champs-Elysees.

On Friday it was time for the first game, all played at the Palais Omnisports de Paris-Bercy. The Bulls won the first game 89–82 against PSG Racing, with Jordan getting 28 points. The contest was actually quite close until the final five minutes.

"Without Michael Jordan, we would have won,' declared French coach Bozidar Maljkovic.

"Who would know?" replied Phil Jackson when told of the French coach's statement. "I guess we would have to try again."

In the second game on Saturday, the Bulls won the title by beating Olympiakos 104–78. Jordan had 27 points in 29 minutes of action.

"Hopefully, the fans were pleased with the little time I was on the court," Jordan said.

In the two games, Kukoc was completely mortal, making just 2-of-15 shots. He was suffering from plantar fasciitis, but also had a certain amount of pressure on him as a returning hero.

The postgame press conferences were a mess of languages, and the players and coaches had to wear special headsets so they could hear interpreters report the questions. The final question of Jordan's last press conference was especially unique, as a French reporter spoke at great length about something, then finally asked Jordan for an autograph for his son. Jordan signed something for the reporter, and as he left the room he looked back and said, "Good question."

And on Sunday I returned home from Paris. Of course, I slept all the way home. I also had a seat in the very last row of the plane, which maybe had something to do with it.

The next day, the *Herald* allowed me to write a personal trip diary in which I thanked my French teachers from middle school and high school for preparing me as well as they did for my eventual visit. It was 25 years after my last class on the topic and I was still conversant.

A couple of weeks after the trip, I received a letter from my middle school French teacher, Mrs. Paquette. She admitted that she barely remembered me, but thanked me for remembering her.

Such was the life of traveling with the Chicago Bulls.

46. Rodman Plays Basketball

Off the court, Dennis Rodman was an intriguing person: pleasant, conversant, self-effacing, intelligent, a pleasure to talk to. On the court, he was often nothing but trouble.

Alonzo Mourning grabs Dennis Rodman during the 1997 Eastern Conference Finals.

I was there at every game in which Rodman got in trouble when he was with the Bulls. I was there when he head-butted the referee; I was there when he kicked the photographer.

But I was also there when he grabbed all of those rebounds for the Bulls. I saw him before games watching opponents warm up. He told me what he was doing and how he studied his opponents in order to know how their shots might come off the rim when they miss.

He knew players who were notoriously short with their shot, and the players who were usually long when they missed. He knew the guys who put up rainbows, which bounce higher and farther off the rim when they miss. Despite a shortened and disinterested attempt at higher education, Rodman was very smart.

He was also incredibly wise when it came to bothering the opposition into mistakes and unsportsmanlike conduct. I hated that aspect of his game when he was with the Pistons, especially when he would try to get the Bulls out of their game, but by the time he was done with the Bulls, I had grown to appreciate just how smart a basketball player and a competitor he was.

Rodman's competitive nature and his gamesmanship were on best display when the Bulls played the Miami Heat. Rodman owned Heat center Alonzo Mourning, whose biggest drawback as a player was that he could not keep his head on straight during games.

Mourning and Rodman tangled often when the Phil Jackson–coached Bulls were playing the Pat Riley–coached Heat. They would hook up in an attempt to get a rebound, and often it was Rodman who would hook Mourning, forcing Mourning to try to disengage himself.

Rodman very famously flaunted a wilder than normal lifestyle. He was clearly not above cross-dressing, best displayed when he wore a wedding dress to a book signing.

Although he was very famously heterosexual, having married Carmen Elektra and dated Madonna, he was also not afraid to at least pretend to occasionally play for the other team.

"Dennis knows there's this homophobia among a lot of players in the league," Isiah Thomas once told the *New York Times*. "So he uses that and everything else he can. It's amazing how many guys fall for it."

Rodman reportedly told players they had nice legs. He waltzed with former Indiana Pacer and eventual Bull Antonio Davis after they tangled up in search of rebound.

But his favorite target was Mourning, who clearly did not take kindly to Rodman's advances. One time, when the two were standing along the free throw lane in anticipation of a charity shot, Rodman patted Mourning on the butt, for no reason, without provocation.

Mourning reacted as if he had been bitten by a rattlesnake.

It was pretty funny.

"Dennis makes it a challenge to take him [Mourning] out of his game," Michael Jordan said. "And Dennis takes pride in getting into Alonzo's head."

47. Jordan Gets Older

In private, in a conversation he knew was not being recorded or would ever be reported, Michael Jordan might have been willing to admit that he thought he would never get old.

Jordan believed nothing could stop him from being the best player on the floor at any given time. He probably still thinks that, even though he just turned 51 years old.

I remember being with him on the day he turned 29, one year shy of 30, which is a benchmark age for professional basketball players. He might have been whistling in the dark with his comments that day, but he seemed fairly well convinced that age would never have an effect upon him.

"I wouldn't say my skills have diminished," Jordan said that day. "There are certain things I haven't been called upon to do as often, and I'm pretty sure people start to equate that with the coming of age. But if I was called upon to average 37 points a game, I think I could do it.

"I still think I could get into the dunk contest and do the things I always did," he said. "But what is the reason? Twenty-thousand dollars? I don't think so."

Jordan admitted he had changed at 29, that he had gained wisdom through age, just as he denied age as a factor in his development.

"I'm wiser," he said. "I've grown up a lot and matured a lot. Mentally, I have advanced myself, just through life. You are never too old to learn. But I don't consider myself old."

48. Dennis Rodman Party

We were in Denver. I love Denver. In exactly the opposite way Seattle suffers from having 300 days of rain a year (which is a lie, but works to keep interlopers out), Denver enjoys 300 days of sunlight a year (and I'm told residents suffer psychologically from not having enough down time that comes from rainy days, if you want to believe that).

One year, on an extra day in town, I attended and participated in a square dance in their very public Larimer Square. Then I walked into the brew pub right down the street and completed what was a very good day.

Denver had a vibrant night life, and no one took advantage of the opportunities presented by that night life like Dennis Rodman.

So it was one night in Denver that Rodman told me and another reporter to meet him in the lobby of the Westin Hotel on the night of our day off to go to a "small" party he was hosting at a nearby nightclub. I am not a "nightclub" kind of guy, but the other reporter wanted to go, and he wanted me to experience it. We both knew it would be something to talk about the next day.

And it was. Dennis and then-wife Carmen Electra sauntered through the lobby a few minutes late, and we all got into a fully stocked limo for a 10-minute limo ride. We ended up in a warehouse district, where a cavernous building had been converted into a stark nightclub. It was merely a lot of bright strobe lights, bars lining the outside walls, and a massive amount of space for gathering and dancing and what-not. It was a scene I was unfamiliar with.

The what-not, it turned out, included gratuitous nudity. A very attractive woman walked up to me and the other reporter (we had been immediately dismissed by Rodman upon entering the club) and showed us her breasts. I laughed, for the absurdity of the moment and the fact that it was very reminiscent of scenes from a John Candy movie.

The other reporter was in his element and I was not, so I left after just a few minutes. But, as I fought my way through the crowd to find the door where I had entered (I failed), I stopped for one moment and just took in the scene. It was not real; it was unreal and surreal and hard for me to grasp—and all at once I thought of that line from *Diner* again.

That was Rodman's life to me.

49. Jordan's Gambling

There remains the belief by some NBA fans that Michael Jordan retired in 1993 because of all the bad publicity he was getting regarding his gambling addiction.

In late May of 1993, as the Bulls were chasing their third consecutive NBA title, the New York newspapers published a story about Jordan gambling in Atlantic City until 2:30 AM the day of an Eastern Conference Finals game against the New York Knicks, a game the Bulls lost to fall behind 0–2 in the series. Jordan scored 36 points in that game, but he spent the entire contest listening to the rabid New York Knicks fans question his dedication and commitment, and he caught endless negative reports from Chicago media that criticized his pregame decisions.

It was the Chicago-area media attack that concerned Jordan the most. Up to that, he could do no wrong in Chicago. In fact, fans were not the least bit concerned about his gambling. It's legal, after all. But some reporters would not let go, and Jordan heard all of the reports. It affected his every moment at home.

Then, in June, came the story that Jordan owed a man in San Diego more than $1.2 million in gambling bets from golf games, and that the man settled for $300,000. He also wrote a book about the relationship, and the heat continued to grow on Jordan.

Through it all, the Bulls defeated the Knicks, then went on to beat the favored Phoenix Suns to claim their third NBA title. There was no talk that Jordan was considering retiring. After all, he was only 30 years old. He had several great years ahead of him, and the Bulls were built to extend their dynasty to almost unheard of levels.

Later that summer, Jordan's father, James, often described as Jordan's best friend, was murdered in North Carolina, and soon thereafter, Jordan shocked the world by announcing his retirement. Almost immediately, it was suggested by rabble-rousing media that Jordan in fact had been given a secret suspension by the league for some gambling sin that went against league rules. Rather than suspend him, the league and Jordan agreed to a public retirement, for which Jordan's father's death served as a viable if extremely unfortunate explanation.

I do not know the truth of the matter. I do know that I took Jordan at his word the day he retired, that he was tired, that life had hit him hard, and that he needed time away.

While all of Chicago moaned and mourned the loss by decision of the city's greatest athletic attribute, I took a different stance, one that got me almost as much attention as the season I did not vote for Jordan for Most Valuable Player.

"Finally, Jordan Can Just Be Mike" said the headline of the column I wrote, in which I encouraged Jordan to stay retired. "What's shocking is that Jordan would ever consider coming back," I wrote.

I figured Jordan had reached the pinnacle of success, but had suffered in terms of the loss of a private life. He was retiring at the very top of sports history, and how many athletes had ever done that? I didn't know I would see it, but I knew I did not want to see him wane the way he did when he played with the Washington Wizards.

I explained how much easier life would be for Jordan out of the public eye. He could concentrate on being a father and a businessman. I obviously envied the fact that he did not need to work another day in his life, even though his "work" was playing basketball.

Obviously, I also did not know he would come back and lead the Bulls to three more titles, climbing beyond the pinnacle he was on in 1993.

When my column was published, a great many people told me to shut up, that the public wanted Jordan to get his rest and then come back. Nobody agreed with me, that retiring at the top of your game was a good idea, especially when it was Michael Jordan we were talking about.

But one person said my column was a good read and congratulated me for writing it.

Jay Mariotti, an opinionated and very controversial sports columnist who wrote for the *Chicago Sun-Times*, spoke to me at some press gathering that summer and congratulated me on writing the one column that stood out among all the others that were written following Jordan's retirement announcement. Most writers said it was a sad day and hoped he would reconsider, while I told Jordan to enjoy his retirement.

Mariotti did not say he agreed with the column, which he did not, but he said it was a ballsy move on my part to write it.

I didn't write it for notice. I meant it, and it got noticed anyway.

But I actually got off-topic here. I meant to tell you about the time I gambled with Michael Jordan.

Which I didn't, really. I can only imagine a day when I could afford to gamble with Michael Jordan.

During the early 1990s, before Jordan retired the first time, the Bulls went to Philadelphia twice a year to play the 76ers, and I never found much in the way of enjoyable activities in Philadelphia. My first trip there, I did all the historical stuff. My second trip there, I stayed in my hotel room.

What I did find eventually is that Atlantic City is just two hours away by car from Philly. (I eventually found out the same thing about Reno and Sacramento).

On more than one occasion, I spent a Philadelphia off night in Atlantic City, which is to Las Vegas what hamburger is to filet mignon.

In fact, one time on the drive to AC with four members of the Bulls' staff, I saw an Unidentified Flying Object. But that's a story for the next book.

What else I saw on that particular trip was Jordan gambling at Harrah's Casino, sitting in the semi-private big shooters blackjack area. He called me in and showed me a little of what was going on, explaining that each chip represented $10,000 and that he was playing two hands at a time. Turns out I did not have the stomach to *watch* someone gamble $20,000 at a time, much less do it myself. So I left.

My little travel party got back to the hotel in Philadelphia at about 7:00 AM, and who walks in at exactly the same time but Michael Jordan. We all had a laugh about our pleasure excursion, and we were still gathered in the lobby when Bulls coach Phil Jackson popped out of a nearby elevator, clearly ready to start his day.

Jackson saw us and asked us what we were up to. My little party group included the Bulls' media relations director, who told the truth, that we had spent the night in AC. After all, we were all adults, gambling was legal, and we did not have to play a basketball game that night. We just had to attend it and write about it or administer it in some way.

Jordan, however, did have basketball responsibilities, and he felt that our answer was not the proper answer he should give to his coach. So he told Jackson he had just had breakfast. Luckily for Jordan, a hotel restaurant was open, making his story possible if not wholly plausible.

I did not write about my excursion, nor did I mention the fact that I had run into Jordan the morning of the game. The Bulls won that night, and Jordan had not done anything illegal, and it wasn't really about basketball, so I kept it to myself.

Until now.

A quick aside: Over the years covering the Bulls, I saw Jordan gamble at cards in informal games on the team bus, I saw him gamble on the timing arrival of luggage at airports, and obviously I saw him gamble in casinos. What I heard, over and over again, was that Jordan never paid off his losses, at least in the informal gambling scenarios. He would just force his gambling partners to keep gambling until he was on the positive side of the ledger, then demand payment.

It was the power of Jordan's will that his teammates continued to gamble even when they knew they would never actually make any money on the deal.

50. The Famous People I Met, and the One I Didn't

Everybody has always wanted to meet Michael Jordan. From every walk of life, from every wealth segment, from every level of fame and fortune, people want to see, meet, and touch Michael Jordan. It's why he was always such a popular choice among Make-A-Wish organizers and the like.

People with some sort of pull, whether it was from fame or fortune, sometimes managed to get a couple of seconds with Jordan at Bulls games. Because I was often in a place where famous people gathered in order to have a chance to meet Jordan before or after games, I often got to meet them as well. Those meetings probably meant more to me than to them, which was not the case when they met Jordan.

One place where I met several famous people was in the Washington Bullets home stadium in Landover, Maryland, which was eventually renamed the USAir Arena. It was the darkest basketball stadium I ever visited; the lighting for the playing area was substandard, and walking up and down the stairs in the building was an adventure because it was so dark. Numerous players complained about how difficult the place was to shoot in because the lighting was so bad.

It wasn't a whole lot brighter in the walkways surrounding the playing area, where the locker rooms were. But it got brighter the day President Bill Clinton showed up to meet Jordan, and although it was on a separate visit, former Chicagoan Hillary Rodham Clinton also visited with the Bulls in Landover. I think she actually gave the team a sort of pep talk before the game. They were playing the Bullets so I'm not sure they needed that.

I did not get to speak to either of the Clintons other than a hello, but I did have a real conversation with Vice President Al Gore Jr., who could not have been more pleasant and accommodating as he waited outside the Bulls locker room to speak to Jordan or Phil Jackson.

We were at the stadium in East Rutherford, New Jersey, home of the New Jersey Nets, the night I met Donald Trump. He was fairly dismissive of the experience of meeting me (everyone seemed to want a photo with the man for some reason), but he is on my list. I only mention it because that's what this chapter is about; I don't consider it a big thrill in my life, either.

There were some famous people who showed up to talk to members of the Bulls at the Berto Center, the Bulls' practice center. One day, Jordan was going to film a commercial with filmmaker and famed New York Knicks fan Spike Lee after practice, and Lee and I talked for a few minutes in the media room as he waited for Jordan. We talked movies, a favorite topic of mine, and actually got into a conversation about the modern movie scripts. (It was at a time when there were all sorts of remakes coming out and Lee told me, "It's because there are no new ideas." I pitched a movie idea about an American sportswriter of

Irish-Scottish descent who follows the most famous team in America, but he did not write it down.)

After Dennis Rodman joined the Bulls and gained more fame than he had ever known, he ended up on *Late Show with David Letterman* a couple of times. When Letterman brought his show to Chicago for a week, he came to the Berto Center to film a video segment with Rodman, and he stopped by the media center to watch practice for a bit. I grew up watching Letterman as a weatherman in Indianapolis before the standup comedy thing took off for him, and we talked a moment about our favorite drinking establishments in Indy. He might have stayed longer than he did in the media room but a radio reporter asked him to do a station identification bumper and Letterman high-tailed it out of our room.

Thanks to Rodman, I was in a limousine with Carmen Electra for a few minutes.

I have mentioned that I met my musical and lifestyle hero Jimmy Buffett on numerous occasions because of the Bulls. He was almost always at Miami Heat games between the two teams in Miami until he got kicked out for some unbecoming behavior during a game. I was backstage on two or three occasions, thanks to former Bulls employee and Buffett fan David Kurland, who worked out an arrangement with Buffett's manager and allowed me and others to take advantage of his deal.

At Bulls home games, famous Chicagoans and famous out-of-towners showed up frequently. Actor and Chicago-native John Cusack was a regular visitor, and I spent one half of a game sitting next to former *Entourage* star Jeremy Piven, who kept me laughing through the game with a running commentary on the athletes.

Peter Boyle, the actor who played Frankenstein's monster in *Young Frankenstein* and Ray Romano's dad in *Everybody Loves Raymond*, was excited to meet the players and willing to meet the writers who covered the players when he stopped by the United Center.

Leonardo DiCaprio came to a game once, and I could have scored huge dad points if I had kidnapped him and brought him home for my daughter, maybe my wife, too. I didn't do it, though.

One thing was for sure: the famous people who were at the game and who showed up on the big video screen during the game would invariably end up outside the Bulls' locker room after the game for the opportunity to spend a few minutes talking to Jordan, Pippen, Rodman, or Phil Jackson.

All except the one person I most wanted to meet.

From 1965 to this very moment, I have been in love with two-time Academy Award–winning actress Sally Field. It was 1965; she was an 18-year-old actress on the TV show *Gidget*, and I was a nine-year-old who had just seen the woman of his dreams.

Everybody who worked for the Bulls knew I had a crush on Sally Field, but I still did not know the answer when Pam Kunkel, the media room manager for the Bulls, came to my courtside seat at halftime of a game in 1997 and said, "Guess who's here tonight?"

I told her I did not know, waiting to hear the name of some celebrity that I could add to my list of famous people I met through my connection to the Bulls. When she said, "Sally Field" however, my heart actually stopped.

I asked Kunkel to point her out to me. She was at center court, 10 rows up. I was one quarter of the stadium seating area away from her. I could not work up the courage to approach her. Besides, I did not want the entire Bulls audience to watch me melt. I knew I would get the chance to speak to her after the game.

I can make this story longer than it will appear here, but suffice it to say I spent the entire second half of the game trying to figure out what I would say to Sally Field when she appeared with her son, who looked to be about 10 years old, outside the Bulls locker room after the game. At that point I had been a professional writer for 20 years, but I could not come up with a script that would convey what I wanted to say in the 15 seconds I would have before she called security. So I figured I would wing it.

I never got the chance. She did not come backstage. I was crushed.

I'm still not over it.

Meeting Donald Trump does not make up for my disappointment.

51. Technical Details

Sportswriting has changed since I got into the business in 1980. In some ways, the change has been for the better; in some ways the changes have been for the worse.

I can tell you it is more difficult. It is also easier.

When I got started in the business, we were typing our stories on word processors purchased from Radio Shack that had only two functions: story creation and filing the story via phone line. Initially, the phone connections were performed by placing the two ends of a phone headset into couplers, rubber "cups" which had to fit just right around the two ends of the headset in order to get the transmission through cleanly. Often, the phone line was interrupted, and even more often, the headset was not properly set into the couplers.

Eventually, our word processors were turned into laptop computers, and those computers were able to send stories by a phone line attachment that plugged directly into the back end of the phone. In many cases early on, there would be one phone for all out-of-town writers in a stadium's press room, and we would have to share that device and time our writing and filing of stories in such a way that the sharing would work out. All of this was done on deadline. Tricky business.

(A quick, funny aside: In one Eastern Conference city, the team had a media relations director who was very persnickety. He expected out-of-town reporters to sit in their assigned seats and use their assigned phones, which wasn't really much of a problem. However, one night, the *Tribune* sent two reporters to a game in that town, and there was only one phone for the newspaper, and they both wanted to file at the same time. They asked to use my phone, which I was not using at the time, and when they did, this media person got very upset. On another occasion in the same city, two reporters who were separated by a third reporter on press row wanted to sit together, and this media person demanded that we sit in our assigned seats. At the next game in that town, we told the Bulls players that we were going to stage an uprising, and between the first and second quarters, we got the media guy's attention from across the basketball court, and then we very demonstrably got up and switched seats multiple times, before sitting in the order we wanted. The players were amused. The media guy wasn't.)

Filing stories at stadiums was one thing; filing them from hotel rooms was another. There were multiple difficulties; getting to the back of the phone to connect the computer was sometimes impossible, or the clip was broken so that it could not be removed so my clip could go in. If a room phone had multiple lines, that completely messed up the transmission process.

We were in Oakland on a West Coast trip, and I was trying to file an off-day story (on the day in between games) from the hotel. The in-room phone connection did not work, and I was trying to find a single-line phone that I could transmit from. I was in the lobby of the hotel with my computer and phone equipment in hand, trying to connect to a house phone that hotel personnel thought would work, when Bulls center Bill Cartwright walked by.

"What are you doing?" he said in that droll, hard-to-decipher voice of his.

"Trying to do my job," I said in a bit of a huff.

"Good luck," he said as he headed to the hotel restaurant for lunch.

In those days, not only did you need a phone line to send a story, you needed an actual phone, because the computer was not yet set up to dial the number. I carried a princess style phone with me for emergencies, and this day in Oakland was turning into an emergency. I eventually found a phone line in the floor of an empty ballroom, where I sat down Indian-style, hooked up everything and sent the file.

Just as I completed hookup and started to send, Cartwright walked by again, saw me on the floor of the ballroom, and smiled. He wasn't smiling with me, he was smiling at me.

Reporters found out back in the late 1980s and early 1990s that the fancier the hotel, the harder transmission could be. Such was the case in New Orleans, when we were there for an exhibition game, and Mike Mulligan of the *Sun-Times* and I were very interested in getting our stories in so that we could go enjoy the nightlife.

We were staying at the Westin Hotel, which was right across the street from one end of Bourbon Street, and I had an opulent suite for some reason (one of the rewards of being a frequent guest program participant, I guess). My room had three different phones, and Mulligan decided to come to my room to file so we could make sure we had at least one working phone for what we needed to do.

Which we did not. Not in my room, anyway. It was a complicated new-fangled, multiple-line phone system and it *would not work* with what we wanted to do. So we separated and scrambled.

After a long search through the hotel, I ended up underneath the desk of a phone operator, connecting to a phone jack that was a single-line connection. The operator rolled her chair away from the desk so that I could sit under the table, connect the computer, and send.

I eventually caught up with Mulligan, who told me he ended up sending his story in from the attendant booth at an open-air parking lot across the street from the hotel.

Eventually all of those problems disappeared with the invention of Wi-Fi, although early on some stadiums wanted us to pay for the use of Wi-Fi and certainly hotels demanded it.

That's the technical aspects of doing the job. The writing job itself became more difficult in 1981 with the creation of *USA Today*.

The national newspaper (which for a short time was challenged by the creation of a national sports newspaper known as *The National*), produced a lot of very short stories and one longer story per section. But somewhere along the line, they also invented the scourge of sports writing, the "notes" sidebar.

"Notes" are little items unworthy of full stories, and often were off-the-beaten path items. This is where a writer would insert interesting statistics (such as free throw defense), silly little references to locker room shenanigans, a rundown of travel adventures for the team, and so forth.

It was just another item that had to be completed, and they usually were requested by editors before the end of the game, and sometimes with an editor's request to update after the game. There were times when the "notes" package was harder to come up with than a game story, and many writers complained about the process.

I'm not sure what legacy I will leave professionally, if any, but I am the man who simplified the creation of the notes package for all writers who cared to listen to me. I came up with a mantra—"Everything is a note"—by which many of my Chicago colleagues now live. And I meant it. If you noticed it, or if you discussed something about the day's events with a colleague, it was a note. There was absolutely no topic too asinine for a notes package.

Today, most professional and college teams provide huge pregame notes packages that offer the kinds of tidbits made for notes packages.

I stopped working for the *Herald* in 2008, so I did not have to suffer the pains of what currently drives sports beat writers crazy—social media. Twitter is the main source of anguish. Before social media, reporters would write a notes package before the game, and a game story after. Perhaps they would update the notes package, or write two different versions of the story depending on their deadlines.

Now, reporters are required to "tweet" numerous times during the game, offering a sort of running game story that is not difficult, but it certainly is additional. Sportswriters are not getting paid more than before because they have more work to do, either.

Sportswriters today also have to monitor the Twitter accounts of the athletes they cover. Athletes sometimes (often?) send out really dumb tweets. Sometimes, they are offensive. Sometimes, they are actionable. It's just an added assignment. It turns sportswriting into something much more similar to a real job.

I'm going to stop here before I sound too much like an old man.

52

Clincher by Kerr, MJ's 39 Oust Jazz
June 14, 1997

The best team in the NBA won the best game of the best Finals series.

Under the first real pressure of the season, at the end of a campaign wrought with a lot of questions and few answers, the Bulls survived the toughest challenge of their five visits to the NBA Finals and walked away with yet another championship.

With an uncertain future, the 1997 Bulls completed a lengthy journey they may not be able to repeat, beating the Utah Jazz 90–86 Friday to claim the title 4–2 in the best-of-seven NBA Finals.

"I didn't enjoy this journey," Bulls coach Phil Jackson said. "It was a very bumpy road through the championship, this night and this game."

"They just keep getting bigger and bigger, and we keep winning and winning," Michael Jordan said. "They [the Jazz] gave us a run for our money. But we persevered and I'm happy knowing that we're the champions for the fifth time."

Reminiscent of 1992, the Bulls' bench pulled the team back from a nine-point deficit and gave Jordan a lead. And reminiscent of 1993, it was the Bulls' long-distance expert who won the game, this time in the guise of Steve Kerr rather than John Paxson.

Kerr, who missed a potential game-winner in Game 4 of the Finals, took a pass from Jordan and made a 14-foot jumper just in front of the free throw line with five seconds left to settle an issue that was, surprisingly, in doubt.

"Tonight Steve Kerr earned his wings," Jordan said. "He's been fighting with himself because he missed that three-pointer. I had faith in him, and I passed him the ball and he knocked the shot down."

Jordan scored 39 points to earn his fifth Finals Most Valuable Player award, while Scottie Pippen had 23 points and earned Jordan's spoken respect.

"We are a tandem," Jordan said. "It's hard to split us up. I'm taking the trophy, but he is going to get the car."

In a losing effort, regular season Most Valuable Player Karl Malone had 21 points in 44 minutes, but made only 7-of-15 free throws and took the blame for the team's loss, both in the game and the series.

"Our guys played hard," Malone said. "We did a lot of good things. We just couldn't do it tonight."

"This was a tougher series than anyone thought it would be, tougher then last year," Bulls guard Ron Harper said. "I'm glad it is over."

Unlike last season, when the Bulls set a record for regular season victories and cruised through the playoffs, this team never looked as impressive until the fourth quarter of the final game.

"This team showed what type of team it is," Harper said. "We always found a way to survive."

The final Finals game was not well played, and belonged to the Jazz at the start of the fourth quarter. With a 70–64 lead, the Jazz had held off the Bulls for most of the game. After three John Stockton free throws, the Bulls found themselves down by nine points, 73–64, and had a lineup on the floor that included Pippen, Kerr, Toni Kukoc, Brian Williams, and Jud Buechler, four bench guys and an all-star.

Pippen made a pair of free throws, Kerr made his first jumper, Utah's Shandon Anderson missed a shot, and Pippen canned a three-pointer. Suddenly, the Bulls were within two points. Both Stockton and Malone missed offensive opportunities, and Kerr gave the Bulls their first lead of the second half, 74–73.

"I think Phil did a good job putting us together on the floor," Pippen said.

Neither team led by more than three points through the final eight minutes, and the Bulls had an 86–83 lead with two minutes left. But Bryon Russell, who gained Finals fame for playing defense against Jordan, hit the surprise three-pointer that tied the game with 1:44 left.

With 28 seconds, the Bulls had the ball in a tie game. During a timeout, Jordan told his teammates to get him the ball, and Kerr told him to keep an eye on Kerr's defender, Stockton.

"I had a feeling Stockton was going to leave me," Kerr said. "I saw him [Jordan] on the bench thinking for a long time, and finally he turned to me and said, 'You be ready, Stockton is going to come off you.' I said, 'I will knock it down.'"

"If he had missed that shot, I don't think he could have slept all summer," Jordan said. "I'm very happy for Steve Kerr."

The Jazz had a final play, but Kukoc tipped the inbounds pass and Pippen dived for the ball and pushed it back to Kukoc, who finished the game with a slam dunk.

"We never had control of this game," Pippen said. "It was like it was going to overtime or the Jazz was going to win on a last-second shot. They gave us our money's worth."

53. When Athletes Asked Questions

The sportswriter-athlete relationship is not a complicated one. The sportswriter asks the questions, and the athlete answers them, when he or she wants to.

Over time, the athlete comes to know the sportswriters who will ask good, thought-provoking questions, and those who just need a quote or sound bite to complete their job. Eventually, athletes develop relationships with the beat writers, who are the only recognizable faces among the media horde when the team is on the road.

Occasionally, with a lot of downtime before games, conversations turn beyond basketball to more personal issues. Plans for off-days, travel difficulties, upcoming anticipated meals, family matters—almost anything was discussed at one time or another over the 11 years I traveled with the Bulls.

At one point, in Detroit, I was with two other writers in a conversation with Pippen. He knew us all well enough that he felt he could insult us, which he did.

"How come all sportswriters are fat?" he asked.

Certainly, the two writers who were not named Kent McDill in that conversation were overweight, but I was in relatively good shape. I was playing tennis on a regular basis, and often exercised away whatever beer I might consume on a long trip. Pippen may have picked up on the fact that he had just called me fat.

"Hey, how come you aren't fat?" Pippen then asked me.

I took that as a compliment, although I'm not sure it was meant that way.

Jordan was always interested in how we spent our off-days on the road. That's how I ended up watching *Sun-Times* reporter Mike Mulligan wager $100 of Jordan's dollars at a casino in Reno; Jordan asked us what we were going to do with an extra day in Sacramento and we told him we were headed to Reno.

Bill Cartwright was a big fan of questioning sportswriters. He really enjoyed asking writers why they wanted to know whatever they had just asked him about. He wasn't being difficult, he just saw the entire process as an irritating game of sorts.

The absolute best question a member of the Bulls ever asked me was in 1993, after Jordan retired the first time. The Chicago Bulls suddenly and unexpectedly needed a shooting guard, and the Bulls general manager had always liked former Bull Pete Myers, so he brought him back to the team in his eighth season in the NBA.

That "eighth season in the NBA" is important to the story.

Myers played for the Bulls in 1986, then began a trip through the NBA and the minor league Continental Basketball Association, as well as Italy. He played for 10 teams before he came back to the Bulls in 1993.

Prior to the first exhibition game of 1993–94 season, about one month after seeing us on a daily basis during training camp and less than a month after Jordan retired, myself and the beat writers from the two metro papers stood in front of Myers' locker at some non-NBA city for the first exhibition game, and Myers realized he had seen us at Bulls' practices back at the Berto Center.

"So, what, like, you guys just follow us around wherever we go?" Myers said.

This was Myers' eighth season since his professional career start, and he was just getting to understand the concept of the "beat writer."

Apparently, we needed some sort of press agent.

54. My Biggest Bulls Story

I got into journalism through the back door. My goal was to be a broadcaster, and I had no plans to ever become a reporter. I had a sense of reporters as diggers of information, and I was more an acquirer of information. Even when I became a reporter upon my transfer to Indianapolis in 1980, after two years as a writer for UPI, I was never motivated to break the big story. In my entire sportswriting career, I think I can lay claim to two big "gets," and although I did nothing wrong, they both turned out to be the result of someone telling me their plans, which they did not follow up on.

In March of 1981, while I was the very young sports editor for UPI in Indianapolis, I was asked to get a one-on-one interview with Isiah Thomas, then the star guard of the Indiana Hoosiers. Thanks to an assist from the IU sports information department, with whom I had curried favor in a very short period of time, I got 15 minutes with the former Chicago prep star.

I had followed Thomas' career from high school to IU. As a kid growing up in Indiana, I was a huge Hoosier basketball fan. I loved watching Bobby Knight coach, although interviewing him was a struggle (he was my first professional one-on-one interview, and he blistered me). I was thrilled that Thomas chose to go to Indiana over DePaul.

By his sophomore year, Thomas had grown weary of Knight's demands upon him, most directly keeping him from becoming the individual star player he knew he could be. It was his job to run the offense in Knight's patterned style, and Thomas was too much of a scorer and showman to work well in that kind of stifling atmosphere.

There were rumors flying all around that Thomas planned to leave IU to turn pro after his sophomore year. Back in 1981, that was a very

Scottie drives to the basket against Jamal Mashburn during Game 1 of the 1997 Eastern Conference Finals.

big deal. Few players had taken that path prior to Thomas, leaving school early in order to turn pro.

It was my job to find out what Thomas had planned.

In a conference room at IU, two weeks before the start of the NCAA tournament which Thomas and the Hoosiers would win, I asked Thomas the question everyone wanted the answer to.

"Are you going to turn pro after this year?" I asked.

And Thomas sighed.

"I don't know how to get people to understand," he said. "I tell them I am not turning pro and they ask me, 'Are you 80 percent sure? Are you 90 percent sure?' I'm telling you, I am 100 percent sure I am not turning pro after this season."

This made national news, and in Indianapolis, the morning newspaper *The Star* made the nearly unprecedented decision to run my story as the banner across the front page. Rarely had a UPI story on a local beat like Indiana University basketball ever been run in that fashion. The headline read:

"Isiah to NBA: 'No, Nyet, Ixnay.'"

Of course, soon after the Hoosiers won that title, Thomas did indeed turn pro, and became a weird sort of pariah in Chicago—the former local hero now playing for the hated Detroit Pistons.

Fast forward to 1997. I am covering the Chicago Bulls, and have been doing so for almost a decade. I was as inside as a sportswriter could be.

The Bulls were in the old and fairly unpleasant Los Angeles Coliseum preparing for a game against the Los Angeles Clippers. It was Friday, November 21, very early in the season, and Scottie Pippen was not playing. He had a bad back, and was also in a contract dispute of sorts with the team. The dispute was, he wanted a new contract and the Bulls weren't going to give him one.

Before the game, I sat down at an empty locker between the one being used by Bulls guard Ron Harper and the one assigned to Pippen. In a rather offhanded manner, just trying to make conversation, I asked Pippen when he thought he would be able to play again.

"I'm not," he said. "I'm done playing for the Chicago Bulls."

"Don't say that, Scottie," Harper said. "Kent will write that."

"I mean it," Pippen said. "I want to go where I can get paid."

"Don't write that," Harper said to me. "He doesn't mean it."

And I didn't write it. But I thought about it.

Two days later, we were in Sacramento. Pippen was still not playing, although he was traveling with the team. I was on press row, just about 10 or 15 minutes before the opening tip, and Pippen came over to me.

"When are you going to make your announcement?" I asked Pippen.

"I announced it to you," he said. "When are you going to write the story?'

"You're serious about this?" I asked.

"Hell, yeah," he said. "They aren't going to give me the contract I deserve. I'm tired of it."

I looked Pippen in the eye and said, "People will be coming after you tomorrow."

"Write the story," Pippen said.

And so I did. I ran into the press room, hoping not to look too anxious, called the office and told them I had a banner story. I wrote it up, explaining Pippen's complaints, and used the quotes from both meetings with him.

I sent that story in, and then did an immediate follow-up, talking in private to Jordan, who said he backed Pippen's decision. I then grabbed

Bulls general manager Jerry Krause, who was on the trip because it was early in the season, and he very gruffly told me, "He has a contract."

I was pleased with what I had written, and had no problems with what Pippen had said. As with the Isiah Thomas story, I'm not the one who said it, I'm just the one who reported it.

I have always had an affinity for Pippen. Although he turned out to be one of the best players in the history of the game, he started out from such incredibly hard and humble beginnings, it was hard for me not to root for him. Playing in the shadow of Michael Jordan, which pressed so hard against him for those two seasons when he had to uphold the reputation of the team without Jordan, he did about as well as anyone could. He expressed human emotions, he wanted respect, and he wanted the money he thought he deserved.

Our next game was two days later in Seattle. There was not going to be any practice on Monday. I was sleeping in my hotel room in Sacramento before flying to Seattle on that Monday when my phone rang. It was ESPN in New York. I was going to be on the Dan Patrick show. Cool beans.

Representing the *Daily Herald* did not engender the same kind of respect that came from covering the Bulls for the *Chicago Tribune* or the *Chicago Sun-Times*. This was evident as Patrick interviewed me. He did not know me, did not seem to know the suburbs had a major newspaper covering the team, and seemed in his manner that he did not believe the story. It seemed as if he might have thought I was trying to make a name for myself by putting out a story that had no backbone.

At this point, I was 10 years into my beat with the Bulls. If I was going to go that route, I would have done so much sooner, like during the years when Michael Jordan was retiring, purportedly because of gambling problems, or with all the other rumors that had no basis in fact and had nothing to do with basketball.

Nope, I told Dan, this is the real deal. He said it.

The next call I took was from Pippen's agent, Jimmy Sexton. I had worked with Sexton on numerous occasions. He was Pippen's agent from the start, and he was the agent for Horace Grant. We had always had a decent relationship. I rarely bothered him and he never really tried to use me.

"Why didn't you call me before you ran that story?" he asked. "I would have told you not to run it."

"You answered your own question, Jimmy," I said. "It's a story. Scottie said it. I would have not been doing my job if I did not go with it."

On Tuesday, November 25, the Bulls had a shootaround practice at the Key Arena in Seattle. Pippen attended, and was the target of a large gathering of reporters, including myself. I stood in the back and waited. I wondered what Pippen would do. I knew Sexton had spoken to him and probably berated him for speaking out as he did.

But Pippen, bless him, stood up for what he said and reiterated his position. He told the world that, yes, he did say he wasn't playing again for the Bulls, and he meant it then and meant it again in front of all those reporters. My story stood up.

Except, as some people like to kid me, it didn't, because Pippen did play again for the team. He did not get a new contract, and he finished out the season.

But that did not taint the story. I did not claim that Pippen would never again play for the Bulls. I reported that Pippen *said* he would never again play for the Bulls. I never said Isiah Thomas was not going to go pro; I reported that Thomas said he was not going to go pro.

So I didn't end up with my own radio show. That's the way it goes.

55. Size Matters

Iwas recently asked to speak to a class at DePaul University in Chicago. It was a leadership class, and I was speaking about the leadership qualities of all of the college and professional coaches I had worked with.

I found out, in preparation for that speech, that I had quite a list of successful coaches on my résumé. My first professional interview was with basketball coach Bobby Knight of Indiana University, who I covered for five years and who I admired for years before that. I followed that with three years covering football coach Mike Ditka of the Bears, 11 years covering Phil Jackson with the Bulls, seven years covering Lovie Smith with the Bears, and I am now on my fourth year covering Tom Thibodeau with the Bulls.

In 1986, after the 1985 Bears ran roughshod over the league and had one of the most impressive Super Bowl victories of all time, Ditka made what some consider to be a coaching blunder. He brought former Boston College and USFL star quarterback Doug Flutie to the team to help at the quarterback position because Jim McMahon was injured.

I attended the introductory press conference for Flutie, which occurred outside the Bears' former Lake Forest practice facility, which was actually the athletics building for the College of Lake Forest. The Bears have since built their own facility in Lake Forest.

As Flutie came to the podium, I realized he really was only 5'9", which is the height I have always said I am. This amused me, and I mentioned my amusement to the reporter standing next to me, who was Dan Pompei, who at the time was working for the *Chicago Sun-Times* and who recently was inducted into the media wing of the Pro Football Hall of Fame. Pompei also had 5'9" typed on his driver's license.

So Pompei and I decided that after the press conference we would go talk to Flutie together to get some additional information for our stories. That was going to be our cover; what we were actually going to do was see if we were taller than Flutie. All three of us appeared to be the same height. Pompei and I both agreed that we should have taken up football.

When I became a beat writer for the Chicago Bulls, I hardly ever had the chance to see if I was the same height as a player on the team. There are very few NBA players in the history of the league who stood 5'9" or under. During my early years, I covered 5'3" Muggsy Bogues and 5'7" Spud Webb, but there certainly weren't a lot of players on the list.

Instead, I was covering players who were sometimes seven-feet tall. Even though that is just 15 inches taller than I am, it sometimes felt like they were twice my height.

One year, my wife Janice and I attended a Bulls' charity function, and before dinner we talked to Bulls center Will Perdue and his girlfriend while we enjoyed our cocktails. Perdue is an even 7'. Our pre-dinner conversation took place standing up, as cocktail party interaction often does.

We probably talked for 30 minutes before we sat down to dinner. As we moved to our seats, I could tell Janice was uncomfortable and I asked her why.

"My neck is killing me," she said. I realized the 5'2" Janice had just spent 30 minutes looking straight up in order to talk to Perdue.

The height difference between reporters and athletes is not usually a matter of discussion. It's understood that the players are often taller, not to mention faster and stronger. We get it. Those that can, do. Those that can't, write about those that can.

What's weird is that the one time it would be beneficial to sportswriters to be interacting with taller athletes, the athletes don't do their part to help out.

Postgame locker room interviews are almost always conducted with the players sitting down in front of their lockers. This forces the sportswriters to jockey for position with broadcast reporters, who have to be close enough to get their microphones within a short distance of the mouth of the athlete. The writers are often forced behind the broadcasters and dependent on the athlete to speak loudly enough to be heard through another human being's body.

If the athletes stand up, everybody can see them. The newspaper guys can hear them. Everybody gets what they need. But most athletes do not consider that. They sit and watch as media members fight for a spot in front of them.

There were exceptions. Michael Jordan almost always did his postgame interviews standing up. The last time I dealt with LeBron James, he did his postgame interviews standing up. That makes it easier for more people to hear the interview taking place. It's a matter of courtesy.

Of course, when the seven-foot-plus basketball players stand up, they force those media members with microphones or recorders to hold their hands up for an extended period of time. For a long interview, that can actually hurt.

Eventually, all interviews will be done by social media, and the problem will be solved.

56. "You Think You're Smart Because You Know Words"

In the spring of 1985, I was transferred by United Press International from Indianapolis to Chicago, and that summer I covered my first baseball game.

I was in the press box sitting next to veteran Associated Press writer Joe Mooshil, who informed me what would happen when we got to the Cubs' clubhouse after the game. Steve Trout was the starting pitcher for the Cubs, and Mooshil told me that no matter what question was asked first of Trout after the game, he would respond by saying, "I just tried to stay within myself." Sure enough, we got downstairs, and stood in front of Trout's locker. He listened to the first question, which was asking him to assess how he pitched and he said, "I just tried to stay within myself," whatever that means.

Part of the task of being a sportswriter is getting decent quotes out of professional athletes, and this is not always easy. Some players just freeze in front of reporters, some don't have anything to say and some don't want to say anything that can be used, whether they are positive words or negative words.

So what you get is platitudes and clichés. It got worse in 1988 with the release of the baseball film *Bull Durham*, where veteran player Crash Davis (Kevin Costner) taught young phenom Nuke LaLoosh (Tim Robbins) all the clichés he would ever need to handle postgame baseball interviews.

When you found an athlete who could handle himself in an interview, you cherished him and in some cases even protected him.

Despite having some difficulty with the hard words, Jordan was incredible in postgame situations. What was amazing about him was that he could say the same thing three different ways, and often had to.

What would happen at a Bulls' home game after the contest was over is that his locker would be surrounded by dozens of reporters, who would gather three deep around the spot where Jordan would eventually stand in front of his locker. Jordan would always get dressed away from prying eyes (I heard a Chicago radio show host talk about seeing Jordan get dressed and it never happened) then he would come to his locker and answer questions.

Jordan was smart enough to know that the first time he answered, the reporters in the back of the gang-bang could not hear him, so when the first wave would retreat, he would entertain much of the same questions again, and he would answer in much the same way, but not exactly the same way. His media training was as good as his basketball training.

For the first three-peat, John Paxson was the other go-to guy, until he got tired of being the only one who spoke when Jordan had his media boycott in the spring of 1993. For the second three-peat, the go-to guys were Bill Wennington and Steve Kerr, who both ended up with broadcasting careers because of their ability to speak. Unfortunately, reporters were still required to hound Jordan or hope Rodman would deign to be interviewed.

Kerr and Wennington chided each other all the time, suggesting that the other sought out reporters and microphones. They called each other "moth" as if they were the moth and the sportswriter or broadcaster was the flame.

Scottie Pippen was also always there, but he was nowhere near as comfortable in front of microphones as Jordan. He tried, and perhaps because he had such a great role model in Jordan he was almost always polite and responsive. His answers were usually shorter than Jordan's, and perhaps not as directed at the question.

The highlight of all my interviews with Pippen over the years had to be the home game when the Bulls pried a victory out of the jaws of defeat with a late-game flourish of points and defense. It was an intense few minutes of basketball in a meaningful game, and Pippen said so after the game.

Or at least I think he did. What he said was that the last five minutes of the game were "dramastic."

That's right. It's a combo word, putting together the word "dramatic" with the word "drastic." Had it been intentional, it would have been genius. I don't think it was intentional. But "dramastic" should be a word.

Jordan very rarely misspoke, but he had that one word that he always got wrong, and nobody ever corrected him. Whenever things did not go the Bulls' way, and Jordan tried to explain what happened, he would finish by saying he did not want to use the excuse as an "escapegoat." Again, had he meant it: brilliant. But I don't think that was the case.

And, actually, "escapegoat" pretty much describes what the word means anyway.

57. NBA All-Star Game

My first NBA All-Star Game was one of the most famous, the 1988 affair in Chicago when Michael Jordan and Dominique Wilkins of the Atlanta Hawks competed against each other in the Slam-Dunk competition. Jordan won, but Wilkins clearly got jobbed by the homecourt advantage Jordan had.

Jordan won the competition because of his famous "leap from the free throw line" dunk. There is a photograph of that moment when Jordan is hanging in the air before he completes the dunk, and I am in that picture, sitting in the stands among hundreds of other spectators. Eventually, that photo was issued as a greeting card with no words inside, and I bought a bunch of them and sent them out as Christmas cards with the sentence "Can you see Michael Jordan in this photo of me?" on the inside.

I'm a funny guy.

I was working for United Press International in 1988, but in 1989 I began my long stretch of attending every All-Star Game. In 1989, it was in Houston, and then I went to Miami, Charlotte, Orlando, Salt Lake City, Minneapolis, Phoenix, San Antonio, Cleveland, and New York.

Over those years, I saw Michael Jordan win the Most Valuable Player award three times. I saw Scottie Pippen win it once, after Jordan retired for the first time. I saw Craig Hodges win the three-point contest (known as the Long Distance Shootout) three times and I saw Steve Kerr win it once.

My favorite memories of those weekends had nothing to do with the game, and I will relate a couple of stories about some of the special weekend events I attended, just to let you know how the NBA treated the media back then. But there is one basketball-related memory I will never forget.

When I was covering the league, the All-Star Saturday had three events: an Old-Timers Game, the Long Distance Shootout, and the Slam Dunk Contest. I had no interest in the Slam Dunk because it was such a subjective event. The Old-Timers Game was mostly sad.

But the Long Distance Shootout? That was an event.

Starting in 1990, former Bulls guard Craig Hodges won the contest three consecutive years, tying Larry Bird for the most three-point titles ever. He lost to Bird in 1986 when he was with the Milwaukee Bucks, but that year he set a Three-Point Shootout record with a 25-point round.

In 1991, representing the Bulls, he gave me the biggest All-Star weekend thrill ever, when he made 19 consecutive shots in the second round of the Long Distance Shootout. The previous record was 11 in a row by Bird.

Hodges' performance was thrilling. With every basket, the crowd hummed and cheered. Every basket produced a louder cheer. Time seemed to slow down. Hodges was "on" like nobody has ever been "on" before or since.

"At that time, I felt like I was the best shooter on the planet," Hodges said to me after the event.

"On the one he missed, he rimmed it in and out," said Terry Porter of Portland, who was the runner-up in that contest. "It's not like he missed it long or anything"

In 1992, he was allowed to defend his title, even though he did not play for a team that year.

For Bulls fans, that is the favorite memory of the Long Distance Shootout. But they have a memory they would probably like to erase.

It was in the 1990 contest in Miami that Michael Jordan had his most humbling moment in basketball.

Jordan did not want to compete in the Slam-Dunk Contest again that year, but the league wanted him involved on Saturday. So he agreed to participate in the Long Distance Shootout.

In his first five seasons in the league, Jordan attempted only 287 three-pointers and made only 58, a 20 percent success rate. It was actually in the 1989–90 season that he started shooting more threes; he ended that season shooting 38 percent from outside. He was getting warm.

Two years later, he would have that dramatic three-point performance in the NBA Finals against Portland, in the game in which he shrugged his shoulders as he ran past fans who were cheering his sudden long-distance prowess.

But in 1990, putting him in the Long Distance Shootout was a stretch, and his performance indicated that.

He scored just five points on the 25 balls of the first rack (and remember, the last ball in each of five racks was worth two points). As of 2014, it remains the worst performance ever in a Long Distance Shootout.

"I was really nervous," Jordan told me after the event. "I was leaving everything short. I tried to correct it but I couldn't. It is mentally very draining."

I was talking to Jordan and Hodges together that year and Hodges offered that the first time in the contest is difficult. He said the blast of music that starts a player's round is very distracting. "Any excuse you can give me, I'll take it," Jordan said.

And now to my two favorite All-Star memories having nothing to do with the game.

In 1992, the game was played in Orlando, and Walt Disney World was a major sponsor and host. I happen to be a huge Disney freak, so I was looking forward to a mostly expense-paid trip to Orlando. I took my wife, Janice, and her sister Margie, who came along to hang out with Janice while I was working.

We stayed at the Contemporary Hotel at WDW, and when we arrived Friday morning, we found out that all the media was invited to a special event at what was then called MGM Studios at Disney World (it's now called Hollywood Studios). That night, we boarded a school bus with all sorts of media and other NBA ancillary staff and drove to MGM Studios, and when we got off, there was a red carpet leading us into the park. Along the carpet were red velvet ropes separating us from fans who were clapping as we got off the bus.

"They think we're somebody important!" Janice said.

Unfortunately I had to tell her that it was part of the show, that Disney had arranged for us to be greeted like stars even though we were not. I should have told her that sort of behavior happens to me all the time.

That night, for about three hours, the NBA had MGM Studios all to itself. All the rides and attractions were operating, and there were waiters and waitresses walking around with food and drink. The restaurants were open as well. It was almost like a dream for me.

The last All-Star Game I attended was in 1998 at Madison Square Garden. This time, the entertainment Friday night was a concert at the MSG Theatre, and nobody would tell us who was performing. There were probably six acts in all, but the headliners were Stevie Wonder and Bette Midler, who performed separately and together. I called my mom as soon as it was over, telling her that I had just enjoyed something that she always wished she could have enjoyed: a live performance by Midler.

There are things about being a traveling beat writer I do not miss, but I appreciated the way we were treated during All-Star weekend.

I had one bad All-Star weekend experience, but it was really only bad because I was doing my job.

When the *Herald* sent me to the All-Star Game, I always wanted to pay it back by providing as much coverage as possible. The year the All-Star Game was in San Antonio, the NBA offered a special halftime show for the game itself, which was sort of a compilation of all the best halftime shows that played in the league arenas during the year.

There was the guy who had his body tied to several human size dummies and they danced together as the Jackson 5. There was the Chinese acrobat. There was Quick Change, a sort of magic trick act that I hope I never find out how they do it.

I thought it would be cool to write a story about some of the acts, but there was really only one guy I wanted to meet. He had an act where he would juggle tennis balls by throwing them down onto an electronic keyboard and thus play songs. Each time a tennis ball hit the keyboard, a note would play. He had to be precise to throw the tennis balls onto the keyboard to play the proper note. As both a tennis player and a former piano player, I found the act fascinating, and our interview was fun.

On Sunday, prior to the game, an NBA representative came up to me and said they had read my story and liked it. But he said that the tennis ball-keyboard guy was cheating, that the electric keyboard was programmed to "play" the proper note no matter where the tennis ball hit the keyboard. Obviously, the talent would try to get the ball as close to the proper key as possible, but if he missed, the correct note would still play.

When my kids started to get old enough to question whether the characters at Disney World were real or if there were people inside the costumes, I always told them, "Don't destroy the magic."

I hate when people destroy the magic.

58. Foreign Influences

For several decades, the National Basketball Association was an All-American sport. Unlike baseball, with its Hispanic influence, and hockey, which had Canada to thank for much of its talent, the NBA and the National Football League were mostly homogeneous from a nationalistic standpoint.

Eventually, Eastern European players started coming over to play in the NBA. Today, the former Yugoslavia and the six countries that were re-created when Yugoslavia broke up have provided more than 50 athletes.

At the same time, the league started promoting itself internationally, and was opening satellite offices in Asia, Africa, and Europe. In response, foreign media started covering the league.

Scottie Pippen, Steve Kerr, Robert Parish, Bill Wennington, Dennis Rodman, and Luc Longley visit with President Clinton after winning the 1997 title. Here, Clinton (who'd recently had knee surgery) compares crutch sizes with Wennington.

Before covering the Bulls, I had some experience with international media. I covered the Indianapolis 500 for several years in the 1980s when foreign drivers began to participate. I also covered tennis, which always had players from European or South American countries.

It was covering tennis that I first got to see my name in a foreign newspaper. A Uruguayan player who had lost the second set of a match on what he perceived was a bad line call seemed to give up in the third set, and I called him on it in my UPI story. The next day, he found me at the tournament and yelled at me for writing that he had "tanked" the match.

I told him that perhaps something was lost in the translation, but he said he had both a Uruguayan and an English copy of the story, and went to the locker room to produce them. He came back and I saw my name atop a story in a newspaper from Uruguay, written in Spanish, I guess. This guy was steamed at me and all I could think was, "How do I get this copy of the paper away from him for my personal archives?"

Because the Bulls were the hottest story going in the 1990s, international media members started flooding the United Center. There were reporters from Japan, France, Germany, Australia, and almost all of the Eastern European countries. Everybody spoke English when they had to but spoke their native tongue when they could.

These reporters were also unaccustomed to the ways of American media. They were strangers in a strange land (NBA locker rooms), which themselves happened to be within a strange land (the United States). They were at once deferential and pushy. They were here to get stories and make their trip to the states pay for itself in terms of exposure and copy.

The players were bemused by the attention. It would be wrong to say they were confused, because their time with the foreign reporters was limited to game days, for the most part. I remember seeing players talk amongst themselves about the reporters who were showing up, discussing what country they were from, and how weird the world had become.

The Bulls' locker room at the United Center, which was twice the size of the locker room at Chicago Stadium, was not big enough to handle the crush of media that were on hand for even the most mundane of regular season games.

Most of these foreign reporters did not travel with the Bulls. They stayed in Chicago and covered home games. But they wanted to "follow" the team as much as possible even when they were on the road, so they often asked me to contribute pieces for their publication.

As a result, I have been published in Japanese and Polish and German. I got the most interesting checks for that work, and I should have photocopied them for posterity.

I do have copies of the stories, and in the European editions my name is clear even though the words are foreign. But in the Japanese magazines, it's only a guess whether they really used my stuff.

One of the Japanese reporters presented me with a copy of a magazine piece I wrote, and highlighted my name in the byline and in the short biography that followed the story. But I can't prove those symbols really represented my name. I was operating on faith.

Bulls general manager Jerry Krause wanted to be one of the first to make inroads internationally, and when he brought Kukoc over from Italy, it was a coup. Kukoc wasn't one of the first Europeans in the NBA, but he was one of the best. All of the others were members of the Yugoslavian national team that could have challenged the NBA Dream Team if it had stayed together.

Instead, Kukoc's Croatia broke away from Vlade Divac's Serbia, and best friends were separated by the ravages of war. Kukoc's family was in danger at home, and he found it hard to discuss it, but you knew that it was on his mind all of the time.

I also want to mention the time I had a conversation with a reporter covering the NBA for an Australian magazine. She was with the Bulls for most of one season, and when Jordan was named the league Most Valuable Player for that season, she attended the press conference at a north shore hotel where Jordan would receive his trophy.

We had previously had only momentary interaction, but on that day as we spoke before the press conference, I realized she was pumping me for information for her story. We sat next to each other during the press conference, and when it was over, she and I gathered our notebooks and recorders and jackets and I said, "Goodbye."

Her response?

"Fare thee well."

There is a phrase you don't hear every day when you are covering professional basketball in the United States.

59. Benny the Bull

I have previously mentioned that I am a Disney freak. I have made my children Disney freaks. I have no problem with the appearance of cartoon characters presented in full body costumes. I refuse to say there are actually human beings inside those costumes. I will not destroy the magic.

The Bulls have one of the most recognizable mascots in American professional sports. Benny the Bull, "born" soon after the Bulls were created in 1966, has always been on the sidelines for Bulls games, entertaining fans and hugging children.

Benny went through a transformation in the 1990s. His original look was kind and soft and cuddly, and eventually he was joined by something that was called "Da Bull" (a play on the famous *Saturday Night Live* skit about "Da Bears") who was wild and angry and threatening. He was there to do all of the jumping and dunking and physical stunts that the soft and fuzzy (and fat) Benny did not do. It was a response to some of the other mascots around the league who did more physical bits, like the Gorilla in Phoenix or the Charlotte Hornets' Hugo.

After I was done traveling with the team, the Bulls sort of morphed Benny and Da Bull into today's Benny the Bull, who seems to appeal to both the children and the thrill-seekers among the fans.

But the cute, adorable Benny was the one my daughter Haley fell in love with.

Haley was born in 1994, at the height of Bulls' hysteria, and the middle of my involvement with them. The team presented Haley with an infant's sweat suit when she was born, and whenever I managed to get Haley to a game, she always looked for Benny.

Which made the idea my wife Janice and I had for Haley's second birthday a brilliant one.

I spoke to a Bulls spokesperson about scheduling a visit from Benny to Haley's party, which was held at our home. The team was kind enough to waive the appearance fee, and when a young man showed up at our house with a HUGE suitcase, we scurried him off to a bedroom where Benny could get ready for his appearance.

It was gift time, and Haley was so happy with all of our dresses and toys. Then, we told her we had a big surprise for her, and that's when Benny the Bull walked out of the bedroom.

And Haley freaked. In a bad way.

We had not thought the experience through, I guess. When Benny appears in front of a stadium of 22,000 people, he has to be large enough to be seen from the seats up in the rafters, but in the voluminous area of a basketball arena, he just never seemed that big. Plus, I knew the guy in the uniform, and he was actually my size.

But when Benny the Bull appears in the living room of a two-bedroom suburban home, he is huge. And Haley was very afraid.

Haley cried loudly, and immediately got picked up and comforted. Benny felt bad, and demurred, and tried to make friends, and tried to help us settle Haley down. Eventually, Haley came around, and the video of her kissing Benny on the snout is a favorite moment in the McDill household.

In 2012, Triumph Books published a book I wrote titled *100 Things Bulls Fans Should Know and Do Before They Die*. I did a bunch of promotional appearances for the book, including one on a morning show from Chicago. The producers of the show thought it would be funny to have Benny the Bull (the new incarnation) running around the studio while I was interviewed.

I did not know this Benny well, but the entire thing went off fairly well. Benny was funny and entertaining, and when the interview was over he gave me a hand slap, and we were done.

At the next Bulls game, in which I covered the team for NBA.com as I do now, a young man came rushing by me and stopped.

"Hey, great to see you again!" he said. And he ran off.

I had no idea. None. This person was a stranger to me.

Then he came running back past me. I must have given him a bit of quizzical look because he laughed and said, "It's me. Benny. We did the TV thing together the other day?"

The magic was destroyed, but my momentary confusion was cleared up.

60

MJ Closes the Deal Again
June 15, 1998

SALT LAKE CITY—History, they say, repeats itself, and it certainly did so this NBA season.

But this was the last time. Never again. History will have to find another story to tell. The greatest sports dynasty of the decade, one of the most entertaining and intriguing stories in

Michael Jordan and Dennis Rodman celebrate after defeating the Utah Jazz for the title. *(Photo courtesy Getty Images)*

sports annals, came to some sort of close Sunday.

With their 87–86 victory over the Utah Jazz, the Bulls claimed the 1998 NBA championship, winning the best-of-seven series 4–2, and celebrated their sixth such title in the last eight seasons. At the same time, they took their first step from present marvel to pleasant memory.

With an uncanny symmetry, the Bulls repeated their three-peat from the 1991, 1992, and 1993 seasons, getting matching titles in 1996, 1997, and 1998. And they won the third one in the second three-peat as they did in 1993, taking a game on a foreign court on a last-second shot before a hostile, and eventually frustrated crowd.

"It was an amazing game," said Bulls coach Phil Jackson. "I

don't know if anybody could write a scenario that's quite as dramatic as that was,"

"This is probably the most satisfying one," guard Steve Kerr said. "It was the most improbable, the most difficult, and it is probably the last."

No one will know for sure for months, but chances are slim the Bulls will return next season in a form identical to the one that took the Delta Center floor Sunday. From Scottie Pippen to Jackson to Jordan, through the constant concerns about Dennis Rodman, including the thoughts about the team's bottom line, only a miraculous turn of events and a 90-degree change of some hearts would allow the Bulls to remain the same team.

Yet, some people hold out hope, and the Bulls did little to settle the issue as they accepted their trophy, accolades and champagne.

"There are still a lot of unanswered questions," Jordan said. "Tonight, it is a lot of sympathetic feelings about this team and where we want it to go."

"If this is the end, this is the only way to go out," guard Ron Harper said.

But the season was seemingly longer than any other, what with the constant concern over next season, and the belief that eventually age would catch up with the defending champions.

"It was mentally draining, more than anything," Rodman said. "The last couple of years, with people expecting us to win. But this year it was more like we had to dig our way out."

If the reign is over, it is fitting it ended with a 17-foot jumper by Jordan with 5.2 seconds remaining. That basket came 13 ticks after Jordan sneaked around behind Karl Malone and stole the ball, giving the Bulls a chance to take the lead rather than, perhaps, need three points just to tie.

"I knew we were going to have an opportunity to win this game, and I wanted to be able to do that from an offensive standpoint," Jordan said. "I was able to knock the ball away. I looked up and saw 18.5 seconds left. It was a do-or-die situation.

"I let the time tick to where I had the court right where I wanted it," he said. "As soon as [Byron] Russell reached, he gave me a clear lane. I stopped, pulled up and had an easy jump shot. Great look, and it went in."

The Bulls had to wait for John Stockton's final three-pointer to miss the target before they began their celebration. The victory brought tears to the eyes of Pippen, who played the game in intense pain because of a sore back that caused him to miss all but seven minutes of the first half.

"I was hurting pretty bad," Pippen said. "I took some treatment and told them I was going to just try to gut it out. I felt my presence on the floor would mean more than just sitting in the locker room."

Jordan scored 45 points, making only 15-of-35 shots but hitting 12-of-15 free throws. Toni Kukoc was the only other Bull in double figures with 15 points, while Pippen made 4-of-7 shots with three rebounds, four assists, and two steals. Karl Malone scored 31 points with 11 rebounds for the Jazz, who outrebounded the Bulls 33–22 and led most of the contest but never by more than six points.

The Bulls got some breaks, including a 24-second violation called against Utah in the first half when Howard Eisley clearly got the ball off with time remaining on the clock. In the second half, Ron Harper was credited with a basket that came after the 24-second clock expired.

But Rodman believed the league wanted the Bulls to lose Game 6 to create a Game 7.

"It was obvious the referees expected us to roll over and die this game so they [NBA] could get an extra $30 million," Rodman said. "Thank God we have the players that believe in themselves."

61. I Hated You!

I arrived in the Chicago area at the age of 11, as I was moving into sixth grade. I went to James B. Conant High School in Hoffman Estates, named after the former President of Harvard and U.S. Ambassador to West Germany. Why, I don't know.

We had a good basketball team my senior year in high school, with a bunch of guys I grew up with. One of our conference rivals was Hersey High School, and their star player in 1974 when I graduated was center Dave Corzine.

Corzine was taller than our tallest player, and he did a good job using his size to rebound and score.

I hated him.

He went on to play collegiately at nearby DePaul University in Chicago, and in 1978 he was drafted by the Washington Bullets as the 18th overall pick. He played two years with Washington and two years with the San Antonio Spurs.

In 1982 he joined the Bulls and played with them until 1989.

When I started covering the Bulls in 1985 for UPI, I wasn't really on the inside, and I saw no reason to let Corzine know I went to his rival high school. Then, in 1988, when I started traveling with the team, I thought it might come up at some point.

That point was in Boston on our first road trip of my first season with the team. After lunch on the day of the game I went down to the workout room in the hotel and there on an exercise bike was Corzine. I got up on the bike next to him and we talked while we rode.

Corzine knew me by name and sight from my UPI days, and he knew I had graduated to being a beat writer for the *Herald*. But he didn't know much else about me until that day.

"So," I said, easing into the conversation with style, "You and I graduated from high school the same year."

"Really? Where did you go to high school?" he said.

"Conant."

"Really?" he said again.

Then there was a pause, and I said:

"I hated you."

He laughed a lot. I told him I got over it, and we talked about the guys from my high school team he knew and was friendly with, and a beautiful relationship was born.

When I worked for UPI in Indianapolis, I got to cover the Indiana High School state basketball championships. Those were incredibly great days. In the early 1980s, high school basketball was still king in Indiana, and I was the state sports editor for UPI. I was a significant figure in terms of coverage of the game.

When I arrived in Indianapolis, I was there to replace the sports editor who had been with UPI for five decades, and he was really a figure in the state coverage of high school sports. I was a newbie, an interloper. I was young.

My predecessor retired in 1981, and I took over. My first tournament in which I was in charge of our coverage was the 1982 state championship. One of my jobs was to conduct a poll of sports editors from the newspapers around the state and compile them for a pre-tournament predictions list.

I also had to supply my own prediction for state champion.

I chose Plymouth High School, a team from the north-central part of Indiana, close to the Indiana-Michigan border. Unlike the other teams ranked highly in the state, Plymouth was an all-Caucasian team, and the tallest starter on the team was 6'2". When the tournament started, they were ranked seventh in the state in the coaches poll compiled by UPI. Which means me.

But I always like an underdog, and so I chose Plymouth to win it all. The only other editor in the state who did so was the sports editor from the Plymouth newspaper.

But Plymouth did in fact win the state championship that year, with a double-overtime victory over Gary Washington. I had to use the bathroom since the end of the third quarter of that game but did not want to leave my seat for even a second. It was one of the most thrilling contests of my career, even through all of the Bulls' championships.

The leading scorer in that game, with 39 points, was Scott Skiles.

In 1986, he graduated from Michigan State University and became a pro, playing with the Milwaukee Bucks. I covered him for a couple of years in the league, but never got the chance to tell him that he was the star of one of greatest games I ever covered.

In 2003, he became coach of the Chicago Bulls. By that time I had moved from the Bulls beat to the Chicago Bears beat, but whenever the

Herald's Bulls beat writer needed a day off, they asked me to cover the team. So I finally had a chance to tell Skiles thank you for that game.

"Long time ago," he said, and he was correct. But those kinds of games stick with you when you are a fan or a player, whether it's in high school or in the pros.

62. Bird and Johnson

I graduated from DePauw University in Greencastle, Indiana, in 1978 with a degree in broadcast communications and was lucky to get a job right out of school, working for United Press International's broadcast department in Chicago. I was the night sportswriter five nights a week, 3:00 PM to 11:00 PM.

When I was offered the job, the man who hired me said, "This will be the toughest job you will ever have," and he was correct. But it worked out for the best.

My job was to take all of the sports stories written by UPI's newspaper writers from around the country and the world and turn them into broadcast stories. What that meant was that I would take a 500–700 word story on a National Hockey League game and condense it into 50–100 words. And I would do that for every NHL, NBA, NFL, MLB, NCAA basketball, and NCAA football game. My short stories were then sent to radio and TV stations around the globe for use in broadcasts, where the stories are shorter by design and due to time constraints.

Back in the day, broadcasters would "rip and read," which meant they would rip the printed stories off the wire machine and then read them verbatim over the air. Writing for broadcast requires the use of relatively simple words that are easy to pronounce, and short sentences so that the

Magic, Michael, and Bird during a photo session for the NBA's 50th Anniversary All-Time Team.

thread of the story can be followed easily by the listener. There is no going back to reread the sentence. Writing in that manner is an art form.

October was the worst month. Every single sport was in action, either in preseason (NBA, NCAA basketball), regular season (NHL, NFL, NCAA football), or postseason (MLB). I had to write a lot, very fast, without the benefit of an editor. If I made a mistake, it went out on the wire.

It was ridiculously hard. It required a commitment to time management, tight writing, mistake-free typing (spell check had not been invented yet), and enthusiasm. It's a good thing I was young.

In the fall of 1978, Larry Bird was a senior at Indiana State University and was leading the Sycamores through a magnificent season. The sports director for the college radio station was John Buckles, who happened to be my best friend from high school, the person who taught me (along with my father) how to play tennis.

Prior to the start of the 1978–79 basketball season, Buckles suggested that when my midweek weekends came around (I usually got Wednesday and Thursday off) that I should come down to Terre Haute from Chicago and serve as his color analyst for Indiana State basketball games. After all, I was the night sports broadcast editor for UPI (sort of). Buckles could trumpet a professional connection for the broadcast, and I got to watch Larry Bird play. So I had the pleasure of calling about eight of Bird's games as a senior at ISU.

When Indiana State played Michigan State and Magic Johnson for the 1979 NCAA title, I watched it from a console television that my college friends and I had carried out of our villa on the beach at Fort Lauderdale, Florida, during spring break. We bought a 100-foot electrical cord to power it, and watched the game on the very tiny screen with the Atlantic Ocean as a backdrop. It was a great night ruined by one of Bird's worse games of the year, leading to Michigan State's 75–64 victory.

Little did I know I would have contact with both of the stars of that game someday.

I saw Bird more than I did Johnson over the years, because Bird was with the Celtics in the same conference as the Bulls and Johnson was with the Los Angeles Lakers in the Western Conference.

In Bird's last season, 1992, I was at the Boston Garden and I saw Bird at his locker trying to figure out the new laptop computer he had. I had never had the nerve to tell him of my background with him, but this was my chance, and I took it. I helped him figure out a maneuver on the screen, then told him the story I just detailed above. We talked a little bit about the days at Indiana State, and the arena in which they played. I felt like I had completed a circle.

I spent as much time as I could around Johnson during the 1991 NBA Finals. He was a different kind of guy. He was happy. He was a great conversationalist. He played basketball in a unique way, designed solely to get the ball into the basket, which I liked.

In the fall of 1991, in preparation for the season following the Bulls' first title, Johnson found out he had contracted the HIV virus. On November 7, 1991, he held the press conference in which he told the world of his affliction. But before he did that, he told his friends, including Michael Jordan.

It was the first week of November 1991, and I was attending a Bulls practice at the Deerfield Multiplex, which was the health club the Bulls used as their training facility until they built their own building, the Berto Center, a couple of years later. A phone in the Multiplex media room rang that morning and I answered it. On the other end of the phone was Magic Johnson's agent, Lon Rosen, who knew me slightly from our contacts over the previous years.

"Can you get a message to Michael?" he asked me. "He needs to contact Magic as soon as possible."

When practice ended and Jordan walked out of the practice gym, I told him Magic Johnson wanted to talk to him pronto. I did not know what Johnson had to say, although I found out soon enough.

Johnson's diagnosis produced all sorts of conversation, and it went on endlessly that season in the Bulls' locker room. There was a lack of knowledge about how the disease spread, and there were players in the Bulls' group who were cautiously concerned about Johnson's return to the game.

The league obviously changed when Bird and Johnson entered the league in 1979. It changed again with Johnson's news in 1991.

It is reported endlessly that the NBA was saved by the inclusion of Bird and Johnson into the league. Their fervor for basketball, their skill, and the fact that they toiled on opposite ends of the country for iconic NBA franchises skyrocketed the league into national and international favor. The arrival of Michael Jordan took that elevated base and shot it farther into the sky of popularity that no one could have imagined before it happened.

I consider myself blessed to have been involved in some small way in the establishment of the NBA as one of the world's most popular sports leagues.

63. Jackson Wanted Rockets

Any Bulls fan worth his or her salt can recite the details of the six championship seasons:

1991—Bulls vs. Los Angeles Lakers. Jordan vs. Magic. Pippen shuts down Magic. Bulls win in five.

1992—Bulls vs. Portland. Jordan vs. Drexler. Trail Blazers outmatched. Bulls win in six.

1993—Bulls vs. Phoenix. Jordan vs. Barkley. Paxson hits the shot. Bulls win in six.

1996—Bulls vs. Seattle. Jordan and Pippen vs. Kemp and Payton. Bulls win in six.

1997—Bulls vs. Jazz. Jordan and Pippen vs. Malone and Stockton. Kerr hits the shot. Bulls win in six.

1998—Bulls vs. Jazz. 1997 redux. Jordan hits the shot. Bulls win in six.

What most Bulls fans don't know is that the above timeline, interrupted as it was by Jordan's short retirement, did not go the way coach Phil Jackson wanted.

What many Bulls fans may not recall is that while Jordan was in retirement and the Bulls did not win championships, both titles were won by the same team—the Houston Rockets.

So, from 1991 to 1998, eight years of professional basketball in the United States, the NBA championship was won by only two franchises, Chicago and Houston. And never did those two teams meet in the NBA finals.

They would have, if Phil Jackson had had his wish.

In 1996, the Seattle SuperSonics were by far the best team in the Western Conference, though nobody thought they were a match for the 72–10 Bulls, and they weren't. But in 1997, the Utah Jazz were the best team in the West, followed by the Houston Rockets and the Sonics again.

The Rockets still had some of their championship roster around, including Hakeem Olajuwon and Clyde Drexler. They also had Charles Barkley on his last legs, as well as Mario Elie and Kevin Willis.

The Rockets, more than any other team, had always given the Bulls fits.

Here is a very little known fact about the Bulls: In the first three championship seasons, the Bulls went 1–5 against the Rockets in the regular season. In the 1995–96 season, the Bulls swept the Rockets in two games (the Bulls beat everybody that year), but then again in 1996–97, the Bulls and Rockets split two games.

So in the five years in which Jordan played full seasons from the first title year until the playoffs of 1997, the Bulls were 4–6 against the Rockets.

Jackson knew this. But when he was asked publicly which team he was hoping would win the Western Conference Finals in 1997, he said it did not matter whether the Utah Jazz or the Houston Rockets won. That, of course, was standard sports protocol. You do not badmouth one team by saying you'd prefer to play the other. It either looks like you think you have a better chance against one team, or you disrespect another by suggesting they would not be a tough enough opponent.

However, when the Jazz did indeed take the Western Conference final series 4–2, Jackson let his real feelings be known in a locker room conversation with me.

"I kind of wanted the Rockets to win," he said. "I would like to see how we would have done against them."

I give Jackson credit for that admission. He wanted to play a team that he knew would give his team a difficult time on the way to victory. He wanted the challenge. He knew not what the outcome would be. He was willing to face the possibility they could not handle the team in the playoffs any better than they did in the regular season. It was a very thoughtful and provocative statement.

Unfortunately, by the 1997–98 season, the Rockets were a mere shadow of their championship selves. They went 41–41 in the regular season and lost to the Jazz in the first round of the playoffs. So Jackson never got his wish.

Instead, we got a repeat of the 1997 Finals with a rematch between the Bulls and the Jazz and it pretty much went the same way. The Jazz had a great two-man team in power forward Karl Malone and point guard John Stockton, which mismatched in an interesting way with the Bulls' shooting guard Michael Jordan and small forward Scottie Pippen, but they did not have the same quality of surrounding players the Bulls had. They had no Toni Kukoc or Dennis Rodman.

Sequels are never as good as an original. And we will never know how the championship Bulls would have done against the championship Rockets.

64. An Indication of Just How Stupid I Am?

So, this entire book has been about my travels with the Michael Jordan–led Bulls for 11 years. In that time, I saw probably all of Jordan's best games as a professional basketball player. I saw the development from Day One of Scottie Pippen, one of the top 50 players in the history of the game. I witnessed the greatest dynasty in the history of Chicago sports. I saw Dennis Rodman naked.

And what do I have to show for it?

Nothing.

To the complete dismay of my sons, I collected no memorabilia from my time covering the Bulls. I got no shoes signed by Jordan, no jerseys, no socks, nothing.

I do have my own newspaper collection of significant moments I covered, including the newspapers of the six championship games. I have a few programs. I have a T-shirt and a hat I bought when the Bulls went to Paris, signifying that I was in attendance at the 1997 McDonald's Championship.

What I do not have, not even one of, is Michael Jordan's autograph.

There is a reason for that. It's a reason I take seriously, although it does nothing to allay the disappointment of my sons.

Getting autographs was against the rules.

Among the many things that are written on the back of every NBA media pass are these words:

"No autographs are allowed during media access periods."

(It also says I bear all risk of physical harm stemming from my coverage of the Bulls. That means if I had gotten injured back when Charles Barkley ran into me, I couldn't sue him or the league. That's why I sit in the press box these days.)

Honestly, it never crossed my mind to ask for an autograph. I was a professional sportswriter. I was there to cover the events of the team and the game. I was expressly NOT supposed to be a fan. Fans ask for autographs. Professional sports media do not.

I have no idea what others have done, but I am pleased that I never stooped to ask Jordan for an autograph.

I was witness to several signing marathons the teams did. The players would line up at the Multiplex of the Berto Center, seated in folding chairs, and for an hour at least, a member of the media relations staff would hand an item to the first player in line, and that item would pass through 12–15 hands until it ended up at the last player. It was an assembly line of memorabilia creation. It was sort of tawdry. I know people who own autographed basketballs find them significant and care for them as if they were gold, but watching the process of their creation sort of took some of the magic out of the concept.

After the items were signed, they would be crated for use by the team for publicity or charity purposes. I have none of them.

I have one item from a championship postgame locker room party, but I can't prove it came from there. After the Bulls beat the Seattle SuperSonics to win the 1996 championship at the United Center, the year my twins were born in the same month, I got hit in the face by a champagne cork popped out of a bottle. I picked it up and pocketed it. I don't know why. It's still in my sock drawer if you want it.

There is one thing I have, actually, hundreds if not thousands of things, that represent my time covering the Bulls. My kids can have them someday if they want them, but don't tell them yet because I want to surprise them.

I have every press pass I ever wore.

Is that weird?

When I first started covering sports as a reporter, back in 1980 in Indianapolis, I was stunned to be in the position I was in. Growing up, I had no intention of becoming a sportswriter. When I started covering sports professionally, I was a newbie, and the press pass validated me. I wore it as a badge of significance. I was somebody.

So I kept the first one I ever got, for an Indiana University basketball game. And I kept all of the rest of them, too. So I have my NBA Finals passes from all the years I covered those games. I have my press passes from all the All-Star games I went to. I have my press pass from the Paris event.

My plan is to wait for my ship to come in (I hope it's some time later this week), and then I am going to retire and in my spare time I will create four collages made out of my press passes, one for each child. I will frame them, too.

Will that make a neat gift?

At some point, I guess I could have picked up the tape that wrapped Jordan's feet after a game. I probably could have stolen a lot of things; I'm a fairly innocent looking guy and was trusted by everyone I worked with.

I suppose I could have made a few bucks along the way. I don't think I would have been happy about it.

65. Freelance Gigs

Because I was on the inside of the greatest sports story in the country, I was offered numerous freelance writing assignments. As a way to keep me from ever complaining about my salary, the *Herald* had no problems with me making a little extra money on the side. It also looked good for the paper to have me contributing to national publications.

I wrote for magazines in other countries, including Japan, Poland, and Germany. I contributed to reports for *Sports Illustrated*, and I contributed to a weekly package of notes in *USA Today* for a number of years.

The *Sports Illustrated* gig was an unusual one, because it came after Jordan's first retirement, and after the magazine famously told Jordan to "Bag It, Michael" when he tried to be a professional baseball player. That putdown caused Jordan to boycott *SI* for the remaining time he was in the league (I don't know if he still holds to that, but knowing Jordan, I wouldn't doubt it. The man knows how to hold a grudge).

But whenever *SI* needed a Jordan quote, they asked me to get it, and I did. One year I remember they were doing a weekly survey of players on a variety of topics, and the best responses among all of their "stringers" got paid, and Jordan was always a good "get."

It again speaks to my relationship with Jordan, I guess, that he knew I was working for *SI* and still he responded to my questions.

I wrote for Beckett, the Texas company that puts out collectible sports card guides. I wrote for Athlon, which once did a magazine on the 50 Best Players in NBA history, and I wrote the stories on Michael Jordan and Scottie Pippen.

I was a semi-regular contributor to a TV sports-talk show on a cable network (when cable TV was exciting and new and not widely watched) and I did radio interviews in Chicago for which I received sometimes very generous dinner vouchers at restaurants in town.

I also did a lot of radio interviews for stations in other NBA cities for which I received no remuneration.

Then there was the day I got the freelance offer of a lifetime.

In terms of notoriety, I was the third man on the newspaper coverage totem pole in Chicago. The beat writer for the *Chicago Tribune* was No. 1, the beat writer for the *Chicago Sun-Times* was No. 2, and the beat writer for the *Daily Herald*, the city's largest suburban paper and the only other outlet sending a reporter to every game home and away, was third.

That was me.

So when the Bulls won their first title in 1991 and the NBA needed someone to write a short history of the team for a sponsorship publicity vehicle, they went to Sam Smith of the *Tribune*. (Smith later wrote the most famous Michael Jordan book of all time, *The Jordan Rules*. I'm in it.) By that time, Smith was no longer a beat writer; he was what we in the industry call a "Bigfoot," covering the entire league. But he was the *Tribune's* most notable Bulls expert.

When the Bulls won their second title in 1992 and the NBA again needed someone to write a short history of the team for posterity for the same promotional vehicle, they turned to Lacy Banks of the *Sun-Times*. He, too, was off the beat, serving as his paper's Bigfoot, but he had been around a very long time, and it was a nod to his extended years of service that they asked him to write the short wrap-up.

When the Bulls won their third NBA title in 1993, and the NBA again needed someone to write a short history of the team for the most notable format in the history of sports, they turned to me.

They asked me to write the back of a Wheaties box.

I was aware that Smith and Banks had done the first two, but I never in my wildest dreams thought the league would turn to me to write the third. I had a lot of very good friends in the NBA office, people I had worked with in a variety of ways even before I became the beat writer for the *Herald*. I had not pissed anybody off in any way. But I knew my place among the pecking order of the media in town. I knew great notoriety was rarely going to come my way, if ever.

But then the NBA asked me to write the history of the 1992–93 Chicago Bulls for the back of the 1993 NBA championship commemorative Wheaties box.

Ask me how many of those I have in my home?

So I sat down and wrote what they asked for, which was approximately 500 words long. They then edited it down to 400 words. This is what appears on the back of the 1993 NBA championship Wheaties box:

> The Bulls appeared old. All they really were was bored.
>
> Fans were worried sick about the Bulls, who won only 57 regular season games after dominating the NBA for 67 wins the previous season. Despite never losing more than two games in a row, the Bulls lost two games to Philadelphia, who didn't make the playoffs, and were beaten three times by the New York Knicks and the Cleveland Cavaliers.
>
> Somehow, the Bulls knew those games just didn't matter. What mattered was the playoffs.
>
> The Bulls swept the Atlanta Hawks in the first round, and made a mockery of those regular season losses to Cleveland by sweeping the Cavaliers in the second round. The Knicks, winners of 60 games in the regular season,

were the next assignment, and they had homecourt advantage in the Eastern Conference Finals.

It didn't matter. With the series tied 2–2, the Bulls beat the Knicks at Madison Square Garden 97–94, chipping the hopes of the rabid New York fans in attendance. The series ended at Chicago Stadium in a 96–88 victory that sent the Bulls to the NBA Finals for the third year in a row.

The Phoenix Suns won 62 games in the regular season, best in the NBA. Again, it didn't matter, as the Bulls won the final series and became the first real dynasty since those Celtics of yesteryear.

And so, after three decades of waiting, NBA fans have a new dynasty to appreciate. Years from now, someone will ask you, "Do you remember that great Bulls team of the 1990s."

How could you forget?

When it was done, I read it and re-read it and decided it was good. I punched myself in the arm the way Brian Johnson (Anthony Michael Hall) did when he finished writing the essay for all the high school students in the movie *The Breakfast Club*.

Then I read it to my sternest, most demanding editor and critic: my wife, Janice.

And she cried a little bit. That's when I knew it was good.

Here is the absolute kicker to the story:

Today I still write freelance pieces for magazines and websites occasionally. My best set client pays me 20 cents a word (that's $100 for 500 words).

The NBA and General Mills paid me $2,000 for 400 words in 1993. That's $5 a word.

For $5 a word, I will write anything you want. Just call me.

66. Jordan Loves History

Michael Jordan was a geography major in college. Did you know that?

I don't remember ever talking to Jordan about geography, but we had a lot of conversations about history. Namely, the history he was making as he plied his trade to the point that he is considered by many to be the greatest basketball player in the world.

That is a subjective matter, of course. Fans who saw Bill Russell or Wilt Chamberlain play on a nightly basis might want to argue the point. Fans who witnessed the greatness of Oscar Robertson would like to have a word or two with the Jordan bunch as well.

But there are some instances where history is not in question. Jordan was the most important player on the best team in NBA history, the 1995–96 Bulls, who went 72–10.

When the Bulls eclipsed the Los Angeles Lakers' mark for best record with their 70th victory, history was made. Whether Jordan knew for sure that he would not have made it without the help of Scottie Pippen and Dennis Rodman and Phil Jackson and all the rest of the roster, I don't know.

But he knew he had made history when the Bulls won their 70th game about an hour north of Chicago, at Milwaukee's Bradley Center.

That night, I was looking for a way to put 70 wins in perspective. So many people wanted to suggest that the league was watered down by more franchises, making 70 wins an easier feat to accomplish.

Some people said it didn't matter simply because the Bulls were so good, they should have gone 82–0.

But I turned to the one man who could put it in perspective for me, from a historical standpoint. Somebody who knew where he stood in the history of basketball.

I asked Michael Jordan where a 70-win season stood in his own personal history of accomplishment.

"Depends on what accomplishments you're talking about," Jordan said in the locker room at the Bradley. "I've got quite a few. You want me to go down the list?"

Yes, please.

His list was:

1. First NBA championship in 1991
2. NCAA championship at North Carolina in 1982
3. Olympic gold medal in 1984
4. Second NBA championship in 1992
5. Third NBA championship in 1993
6. Second Olympic gold medal in 1992
7. Draft day in 1984
8. 70 wins

"Right now, I really don't see the importance until I step back and say 'Hey, that was a major accomplishment,'" Jordan said. "If we win the championship this year, I'm pretty sure it will rank in the top three."

So, I guess that pushes 70 wins down to No. 9. Unless the fifth championship and the sixth championship push it down to No. 11.

When winning 70 games in an 82-game schedule does not make your top 10 of personal sports accomplishments, that's a career.

Among the things Jordan did not list were his five Most Valuable Player awards, his All-NBA and All-Defensive team selections, his three All-Star Game MVP awards, his 10 scoring titles, and his single selection as Defensive Player of the Year.

It is a measure of his greatness that he has so many accomplishments that those awards don't make his top 10.

I wonder today if you asked him for a top 10, what he would select?

67. Injuries

After a childhood filled with illness related to allergies and severe asthma, I started running cross-country in eighth grade and ran all through high school before switching to tennis. The running built up my lungs and saved my life, at least from a standard of living sense. I credit my cross-country coach, Jack Ary, with improving my life dramatically.

One thing I was taught in cross-country was that there is a difference between pain and injury. You can't run long distances without enduring pain, which I did. But I was never injured, not to the point where I stopped running.

In order to run long distances, runners have to deal with "the wall," which is the pain that comes from oxygen debt. You have to run through the wall, to a place on the other side where either the pain subsides, or you just learn to ignore it, like you ignore your co-worker's humming habit.

The difference between pain and injury is a significant part of being a professional athlete. In short, almost every professional athlete is in pain during a game—whether it is legs or feet or lungs or head, few players participate in professional sports without experiencing some discomfort during almost every game they play.

But injury, that's something that does not go away with a minute's rest. That's something that causes players to miss games. Players hate injury, and will often hide the fact they are injured as long as possible. They certainly don't like to talk about it.

By the time the 1992–93 season rolled around, everyone was injured. Playing 100 games a year between exhibitions, the regular season and the playoffs all the way through the title round not only extended the bodies of the championship Bulls, it cut short their summer break. Playing to the end of June, then celebrating for a month, and suddenly it was time for them to get in shape again for the start of training camp the first week of October.

So it was no surprise when I got to the Multiplex one day in October of 1992 and found nobody practicing. Everybody was hurt, and John Paxson was the hurtest (which means "most hurt").

Being a point guard, it's not surprising that Paxson's problem was his knees. I asked him when was the last time he played a game without pain, and he did that head tilt that indicates the question required deep thought.

"I really don't know," Paxson said. "I have had this knee problem for years."

But point guards don't have the problems centers and forwards have. There are more moving parts to a person who stands 6'8" or taller, and they are required to jump all the time, which causes significant impact on every joint below the waist.

Phil Jackson was slightly bemused as he took stock of his wounded players.

"You have to play hurt," Jackson said. "One of the most important keys is to play through an injury while you are undergoing therapy."

The most popular person after an NBA game is the locker room attendant in charge of ice. Everyone puts ice on some part of their body after a game. Shoulders, knees, feet, ribs—it's a good thing ice is an inexpensive treatment option.

The problem that existed in pro sports for so many years when all of the leagues were in their infancy was that athletes would play even when they were really injured, for fear of losing their position or playing time when they were healthy.

It falls to the athletic trainer to determine who is in pain, who is injured, and who is lying about being in pain or being injured.

"Pain is such a subjective thing," Bulls trainer Chip Schaefer said. "No one knows what someone is experiencing. But it does amaze me when we play four games in five nights, and I know someone's knee is real sore and they put on the uniform, get taped, and go out and play, still trying to perform at the best level they can. I admire them for not talking about it."

Scottie Pippen had frequent ankle problems and chronic back pain. He also had the stigma of being judged "soft" when he failed to play well in Game 7 of the Eastern Conference Finals against Detroit when a severe migraine dropped him like a sack throughout the game.

So when he found out that his migraines were caused by vision problems, then came up with constant back pain, he was not going to let it keep him off the floor.

"Once you get on the court and play with it, it doesn't faze you as much as when you have to deal with it off the court," Pippen said. "There are so many goals out there you want to accomplish. That's why I wouldn't take time off."

"Deep down, coaches want players who will play through injuries," Paxson said.

Jackson, who as a coach was always more considerate about the mental aspects of the game than other coaches, said that players who prove they can tough it out will benefit.

"It builds better people and teams," Jackson said. "When you live through it as a younger player, you can really notice you can play through anything."

"I have worked with coaches that don't ask the players how they feel and try to communicate through me," Schaefer said. "But Phil does a good job of keeping the lines of communication open. It helps when the coach cares enough to ask."

Because I was lucky enough to start my time as a beat writer before all the new arenas were built (I worked in Chicago Stadium, the Spectrum in Philadelphia, Market Square Arena in Indianapolis, the Boston Garden, et al) I often got to watch as players were prepared for games (today that's almost impossible because the training rooms are separated from the locker room). One day, in the midst of a pregame conversation with Michael Jordan, I happened to look down at his feet just before Schaefer began to tape him up.

What I saw was something I would not wish on anyone. Jordan, a good-looking man with a great smile and more talent at his chosen sport than anyone before or after him, had really ugly feet.

"Man, your feet are really ugly!" I said.

"Let me see your feet," Jordan said in defiance. So we compared. My feet, by comparison, were much smaller and relatively gorgeous.

"That's what happens," Jordan said. "Go out there and look at the other guys. Nobody can play basketball and have pretty feet."

In 1994 or thereabouts, the NBA changed its rule regarding roster size and injury reports. Teams were no longer allowed to keep more than 12 healthy players. Other players could be kept on the roster if they were injured, but any player placed on the injured list had to miss at least five games. Those rules no longer apply, as teams are allowed to keep 15 players on their roster but can only have 12 active for each game.

When the rules were changed, players were kept around with injuries of a nearly undetectable nature, so that teams would not have to release someone and make that person available to other teams. There was one injury that kept coming up, and was a relatively new term to most of us who covered professional sports—plantar fasciitis.

Plantar fasciitis is an inflammation of the plantar fascia, which is a thick layer of tissue that surrounds the heel. Plantar fasciitis is pain that erupts in the heel and the inner part of the foot. It makes it hard to run without pain.

By 1993, everybody was coming down with plantar fasciitis. Since it was an injury that was impossible for me to see (nobody could show me their plantar fasciitis), and since the Bulls were going through a rash of plantar fasciitis, with a player conveniently coming down with a case of plantar fasciitis just as another player got healthy from it, that I coined a phrase.

I called it "plantar facetious." It's funnier as a spoken joke than a written one.

I used that joke a great deal in 1997, when the Bulls were playing for their fifth title and second in a row, the first one they played against the Utah Jazz.

Bulls center Bill Wennington, a player I had a very good relationship with (and one with whom I ghost-wrote a book titled *Tales From the Chicago Bulls Locker Room*, about his days with the team), did not play in the 1997 playoffs because of plantar fasciitis. Instead, the Bulls played Luc Longley, veteran Robert Parish, and Bison Dele in the middle.

But his injury did not keep Wennington from enjoying himself. When the Bulls played the Miami Heat in the Eastern Conference Finals, Wennington and I one night ended up in Dan Marino's sports bar/restaurant competing against each other on side-by-side electronic wave riders, the ones where you sit on a "bike" and maneuver it over waves simulated on a video screen in front of you.

As Wennington took an early lead in one race, I yelled over to him, "Aren't you supposed to be injured?" I snuck a quick look at him and he was up on his feet, hunched over the handlebars, and his plantar fasciitis (plantar facetious) was not bothering him one bit.

He did use his injury as an excuse to stay out of a Dance Dance Revolution competition with me later that night.

68

A Bond with Sports That Lasts a Lifetime
January 1, 1988

My father, K.B. McDill, died December 19 of liver cancer at the age of 68.

If there was one thing he and I had in common, it was an interest in sports. When I was growing up, he and I could talk about our favorite teams, which were usually the ones connected with St. Louis, where he grew up and I was born.

It was the baseball Cardinals for a long time, then it became the Indiana Hoosiers basketball team when we lived in Indianapolis. That was back when Branch McCracken was coach, and we talked a lot about that team during the first few years of Bobby Knight's regime.

My father grew up in what was then a very small town about 30 miles outside of St. Louis called Eureka, Missouri. The town was so small that everyone participated in every sport, and despite never standing taller than 5'7", he played baseball and basketball at Eureka High School.

I remember him telling me about his one trick play in basketball. When his team needed to inbound the ball against a full-court defense, a teammate would have the ball out of bounds and he would walk up to him, staying inbounds, and say, 'Let me throw it in.' The teammate would give him the ball, effectively inbounding it, and my dad would turn and dribble it upcourt.

For years, my father and I shared a dislike for professional basketball, which was the way everyone in Indiana felt in the 1960s and '70s. Nobody ever took the Indiana Pacers seriously, not when you could cheer for the Hoosiers, or Notre Dame if you were so inclined.

We moved to Chicago in 1967, and my father adopted the Chicago Bears as his team. We stayed in touch with the baseball Cardinals, although he took a liking to the Cubs, which never passed down a generation.

My father affected my own sports career at an early age. A left-hander himself, he desperately wanted me to be left-handed, and according to my mother, started with me at an early age, pushing balls toward my left hand so it would develop.

I eventually became ambidextrous, which my father said meant that I couldn't do anything with either hand. He was correct in terms of golf, but I can play tennis either way, and

I'm the only person I know of who has bowled a 200 game left-handed and right-handed. He's responsible for that.

I was probably an athletic disappointment to him as a child, because I was sickly, suffering from significant asthma. So when I became involved with the cross-country team at Conant High School and had a modicum of success as a freshman, he was extremely pleased.

After my junior year, when many of my friends were working after school and making money I didn't have, my father told me to stay with the cross-country. It was the right thing to do, and one of two pieces of advice he ever gave me, the other being about going through fraternity rush in college, another decision that worked out well.

My father was responsible for my initial interest in tennis, although he lost interest himself when I got good enough to beat him. And, once he retired from the working world, we were able to talk golf, which I had abandoned and he had taken up (and played right-handed).

When I started out as a sportswriter, he worried whether I would be able to make any good money at it. When I broke my first story, working for UPI in Indianapolis, he understood the draw of the gig.

When I started covering the Bulls for the *Daily Herald* in 1988, he deemed me a success and became a bigger Bulls fan. That was about the time a lot of other people became Bulls fans.

The day in November when he was diagnosed with liver cancer, I told him I was coming down to visit him, and he told me to bring a pocket Bulls schedule with me.

On the day he died, I was in his home in Florida, going through some paperwork and old photos. Then I noticed the Christmas cards he had received, and one Christmas present.

It was the gift we had sent him, the one thing he said he wanted.

It was a polo shirt, red and black stripes, with a Bulls logo on the breast.

If I had become a carpenter, I wonder if he would have asked for a hammer.

69. Throwing Chairs

I am not one to toot my own horn. I wish I was. It probably would have helped me in many ways in life.

But I'm more the kind of guy who wants to be recognized for what he is doing rather than yelling out, "Hey, look what I am doing!"

But I am now going to state my three distinctions in life, two of them related to my coverage of the Chicago Bulls from 1988 to 1999:

1. I am one of the few people in the world who has bowled a 200-plus game right-handed AND a 200-plus game left-handed.
2. I am the only beat writer who covered all six Bulls championship teams.
3. I am the only writer, and perhaps only person, who was present the day Bobby Knight threw a chair AND the day Scottie Pippen threw a chair.

Go ahead. Beat that.

Throwing chairs is not a regular occurrence in basketball games. It's really frowned upon. You aren't supposed to throw anything onto the court. It's a quick way to get out of the game, and perhaps out of the next game your team plays.

But two of the most famous chair throws not involving professional wrestling were performed by Indiana University basketball coach Bobby Knight and Bulls forward Scottie Pippen.

Here are those stories:

February 23, 1985—I am one month away from moving to Chicago to become the assistant sports editor for the Midwest Division of United Press International. At the time of the game, I was the Indiana State Sports Editor for UPI, and I was covering the Indiana Hoosiers playing the Purdue Boilermakers at Assembly Hall in Bloomington.

I loved covering college basketball more than anything, but I always knew that when I was covering a game involving Knight that anything could happen. On this night, he actually did "anything."

Early in the first half, after the Boilermakers took an early lead and several fouls were called against the Hoosiers, Knight finally went too far, and earned a technical foul with about 15 minutes left in the half. That further enraged Knight, who reached for a folding chair which was part of the Indiana bench, and threw it onto the court.

Ironically, he sort of threw it in my direction. If it had continued on its path, and climbed a few rows up, it would have hit me.

I worked for a wire service for which the motto was "There is a deadline every minute." In real life, the deadline was every second. This was a huge story and I had to get the story out as fast as possible.

I turned to look at my competitor from the Associated Press, a man I had worked with (against) for the past five years, and he looked at me as if he had just seen the apocalypse. We both knew we had to get the story out as quick as possible, so we both grabbed our phones as fast as we could.

What we did then was very old school. We each dictated stories to our news desks in Indianapolis. There was a bulletin—"Knight Throws Chair"—followed by a one-paragraph urgent, followed again by a three-paragraph update on the story.

It was immediate, as immediate as stories could be back then. It was at once intense and hilarious. Knight had finally reached a new boiling point.

Fast-forward to:

January 24, 1995—The Bulls are in their second season without Michael Jordan. Scottie Pippen is their leader on and off the court. His role is to try to get the Bulls back to championship contention without the man who got them there in the first place, Jordan.

Pippen suffered a horrible defeat in 1994 when the Bulls were eliminated by the New York Knicks in the semifinal round of the Eastern Conference playoffs. Two very questionable calls by a veteran NBA referee ended Pippen's best shot at proving that he, too, could lead a team to a championship.

By the time the 1994–95 season rolled around. Pippen had other concerns. He wanted to be traded to a team that would give him a long-term and lucrative contract. He had fought with the Bulls over more money without success, and regularly talked about leaving the team via trade. The Bulls were not going to grant his request without getting value in return, and how do you get value on a guy who was eventually deemed one of the top 50 players in the history of the NBA?

The Bulls were at home playing against the San Antonio Spurs, and before the game I sat down with Pippen at his locker to discuss his continued issues with Bulls management.

"I might have to do something to make them get rid of me," Pippen said with a smile.

I thought of those words as Pippen received a technical foul for arguing that future teammate Dennis Rodman, just a few months away from joining the Bulls, was camped out in the lane and should be whistled for a three-second violation. When the technical came, Pippen went nuts, and immediately earned a second technical foul, forcing him to leave the game.

But he wanted to be remembered, and he wanted to make sure his point was made. So he grabbed a chair (not a folding one this time) from the empty seats occupied by fans and kind of slid it across the floor with anger, just not as much as Knight showed 10 years earlier.

Pippen, who said he never swore in his argument with the refs, was suspended for one game and fined a bunch of money for his actions, and was more apologetic for his actions than Knight, who was not apologetic at all.

"I have never been madder in my life than I was," Pippen said several days after the event (he took a few days off to cool down). "It really hurts me to ever get kicked out of a game. But especially that game because it was against a good team with one of the league's best players. We had a good chance to win and my being ejected hurt my teammates. They didn't deserve that."

Pippen said he was not reacting to his current relationship with the Bulls about money.

"I feel bad for throwing the chair," he said. "But I was frustrated. I wish the chair had been the referee instead."

If it had, of course, I would be the only writer who was witness to a coach throwing a chair AND a player throwing a referee.

70. Comparing Incomparables

There is something about the Chicago Bulls of the 1990s that would be very difficult to duplicate. Yes, I'm talking about winning six titles in eight years, but I am also talking about how they did it.

The first three championships were won from 1991–93 with Jordan and Pippen and Horace Grant and Bill Cartwright and John Paxson and B.J. Armstrong. Phil Jackson was the coach, and Jerry Krause was the general manager, and I was there, too, of course.

Here comes the amazing part. The Bulls won three more titles from 1996–98 with Jordan and Pippen and an entirely different cast of characters—Dennis Rodman and Luc Longley and Ron Harper and Toni Kukoc and another variety of second-stringers who helped share one of the greatest teams in the history of the NBA.

Krause is not a public figure in Chicago, because fans were taught to hate him from his battles with Jackson and Jordan. But Bulls fans should praise him endlessly for his ability to form not one but two championship teams around Jordan and Pippen.

When the 1995–96 team went 72–10, they obliterated the record for most wins in a season. They were so dominant that the *Herald* stopped asking me to write game stories. What was the point? It was just one night after another of the Bulls dominating on offense and defense. The only thing that changed for most of the games was the final margin.

So for most games I was required to come up with a feature story rather than a game story. Previously, feature stories were left for those days when the team did not have a game to play. But now I was forced to find something other than the game to write about and I had to do it 72 times in one season.

When the 1996–97 season rolled around, we knew the Bulls were not going to match the 72 wins. But we also knew that they were very likely to win their second championship in a row; nobody in the Western Conference was going to be a real challenge to them, and the Eastern Conference was their playground.

The 72–10 team was so dominant that it did something I might have thought impossible; it made Chicago fans forget, at least a little bit, about how great the first three-peat team was. It was almost like the first three championships were a stepping stone to the greatness of the 1995–96 team and those over the next two seasons.

In Cleveland's new downtown arena in early 1997, in the winter following the remarkable performance of the 1995–96 team, I walked into the locker room and found Jordan by himself. I had waited for the proper moment to ask Jordan a question that had hung in my mind since the end of the '95–96 season.

So I asked him: "If this current team played the team from the first three-peat, who would win in a seven-game series?"

It was one of those questions nobody else had ever asked and I knew that if Jordan would answer, it would create headlines at home, which he did and it did.

So Jordan went through player by player and decided that the 1991–93 three-peat team was better than the team that won 72 games and would go on to win two more titles.

"I think the three-championship team was a better team," Jordan said. "That's from a systematic look at it."

At that point, he and I went position-by-position to compare. It was a game that Bulls fans had played in bars and on playgrounds over the previous year, and I was getting to play it with Jordan himself.

We talked about the centers, Bill Cartwright versus Luc Longley, two players with whom Jordan had either difficulty (Cartwright) or disdain (Longley).

"Bill Cartwright was not as dominant an offensive player, and I think they both [Cartwright and Luc Longley] have a defensive presence," Jordan said. "But I think Bill had more because he was an aggressive player."

We talked about the off-guard position, which was Paxson in the first three titles and Harper in the second. Paxson and Jordan spent many years together as teammates, and Harper was a longtime foe of Jordan's before joining him on the Bulls.

"[John] Paxson, with his capabilities as a shooter, was a different player than Ron Harper, who is more defensive oriented," Jordan said. "You are going to lose some defense [with Paxson] but you are going to gain some offense. I'm not saying Paxson is better than Harper, but he fit into the system because he was around longer than Harper."

Then we talked about power forwards. It was Horace Grant, a young buck when he won titles with the Bulls, against Rodman, who was an established star forward and a whack job when he was with the Bulls.

"Certainly Dennis is going to have the rebounding, but Horace brings rebounding, defense, and offensive capabilities," Jordan said. "And you could count on him every night, you know he is not going to go off the deep end. You don't have to contain him or his personality."

That left two comparisons I was dying to hear—young Jordan against old Jordan and young Pippen against old Pippen.

"I think it's a standoff, Michael Jordan vs. Michael Jordan," Jordan said. "My knowledge of what I am capable of doing now overcomes some physical disabilities I have now.

"Scottie was more athletic, physically healthy in those [first three-peat days] days, but his confidence is strong here in this era because of my years away from the game. I think it is a standoff with those two as well."

Talk about a great bar conversation. I wonder how many Bulls fans would agree.

71. This Is the End

Have you ever had a favorite TV show that was nearing the end of its run, and it has a terrific wrap-up episode to finish a season, and then there is a rumor that it may come back for another year, and it had not yet been truly cancelled, and you had to hang on to hope it was going to return, only to have your hopes dashed in the end?

That's kind of what the summer of 1998 was like.

Carrying the television series analogy a little further, what we got in the 1998–99 season was something like what happened when the TV show *M.A.S.H.* came to an end—we got *After M.A.S.H.*

Or for younger readers, the 1998–99 season was like what happened when the TV Show *Friends* came to an end—we got *Joey.*

The summer of 1998 was one of the most bizarre summers for anyone associated with the Chicago Bulls, including me.

When the Bulls completed their second three-peat championship by defeating the Utah Jazz yet again, it was certain that change was coming. But no one knew for sure what that change would be, or how all-encompassing it would turn out to be.

What was known right away was that Phil Jackson was not coming back to coach. His relationship with Jerry Krause had deteriorated to the point where they had to have a divorce. When Jackson signed a one-year deal to coach the team for the 1997–98 season, Krause made

Michael Jordan hits the game-winning shot over Bryon Russell in Game 6 of the 1998 Finals. *(Photo courtesy Getty Images)*

it clear it was a one-year deal and that there would not be another, and he held true to his word.

But the saga of who the next coach would be was just completely bizarre, and a tale for a few paragraphs below.

Michael Jordan, Scottie Pippen, and Dennis Rodman, among others, were at the end of their contracts. It was almost as if it was predestined to be a three-year run. At the same time, the NBA and the NBA Players Association were at the end of their collective bargaining agreement, and no new deal appeared in the offing, at least on July 1, 1998.

As I said from the start, I never intended to be a reporter. I was, and am, a writer first and foremost, a storyteller second, and an interviewer third. Those are my best skills.

But in the summer of 1998, I had to put my big-boy reporter shoes on and deal with a lot of non-basketball stuff, like CBA negotiations and coaching mysteries and promises made and broken.

The gist of the summer boils down to these points:

1. Michael Jordan was not going to return to play for the Bulls if Jackson was not coach; however,

2. The Bulls believed that if they could offer Jordan the chance to select his own coach, he would do so and remain with the team, however,

3. Jordan also made it clear that he would not return to the Bulls unless they made good on a hefty offer to Pippen, however,

4. The Bulls could do nothing until a new CBA was signed, a new salary cap was determined, and the entire league would move forward.

The truth behind all of those points is that almost none of them were true, in the 100 percent sense.

Jordan was not going to come back to the Bulls, no matter what they offered Pippen. He was tied to Jackson, as far as his career with the Bulls was concerned. The Bulls knew that, which is why they hired Tim Floyd to coach the team, only they didn't really, except they really did (more to that story a few paragraphs down).

From the time the previous season ended to the time the new CBA was signed in January of 1999, there were endless stories, some by me, about the Bulls waiting to see what Jordan would do once the CBA was signed. Every time Jordan made a public appearance in Chicago, I was there, to document the fact he wasn't saying anything.

I had to attend a couple of player's union sessions and votes, held in Chicago because it's centrally located and O'Hare Airport is such an easy meeting place. I had to write about cancelled games, and players trying to stay in shape, and most of my stories had unanswerable questions in them.

When preseason games got cancelled, I missed my chance to go to Greenville, South Carolina, for one of the Bulls' games, although I think Greenville was more upset about it than I was. Once the start of the regular season got cancelled, and it appeared clear the Bulls were not going to have any of their top three available players back, we had to start making up stories about what the Bulls' roster would look like once the season started, if it did.

At the time, the Bulls had only five players under contract—Toni Kukoc, Ron Harper, Randy Brown, and two newbies, including a rookie draft pick they could not sign until the CBA was agreed to. So the *Daily Herald* and I put together a graphic of every free agent in the league, and asked our readers to select a team for the 1998–99 Bulls.

It was a credit to the readership of the *Herald* that they did not just pick the best players on the list, knowing perhaps that no team could just get the seven best players. The CBA and salary cap would not allow it. Who the readers ended up voting for were Antonio McDyess,

Damon Stoudamire, Jayson Williams, Rik Smits, Tom Gugliotta, and two former Bulls, Will Perdue and Jason Caffey (in terms of Caffey, it shows why NBA teams do not let fans pick their free agent signings).

We ran a series of my former stories about Michael Jordan's greatest moments, saying goodbye even before it was official.

And I spent a little time getting to know the next coach of the Bulls, Tim Floyd.

On July 23, the Bulls announced that Floyd had been signed as director of basketball operations with the team. They could not name him as coach because they held out hope that A) Jackson would unretire, knowing that his return would include Jordan's return or B) Jordan would hold to his oft-stated plans to play only for the Chicago Bulls his entire career, make a triumphant return and name his own coach (who apparently would work under Floyd, who would work under Krause).

"The position of head coach of the Chicago Bulls is not going to be filled at this time," is what Bulls owner Jerry Reinsdorf said. "It will be left open, perhaps until the end of the lockout. During that time, if Phil Jackson changes his mind and decides to return, Michael can have the coach that he and we have always wanted him to have."

Is that weird, or what?

For six months, NBA fans and Bulls fans were held in limbo.

What was I up to?

My wife, Janice, was preparing to deliver our fourth child, Kyle, who was born in October of 1998. Our oldest was four years old, my twins were two, and I was trying to make sense of home life while trying to make sense of the future of the Bulls.

When the previous season ended, I sort of jokingly announced that my professional life had ended at the age of 42. I knew I would never get to do again what I had done for the previous 10 years—cover one of the greatest basketball teams of all time.

Eventually, as is always the case, the NBA and Players Association came to an agreement in late January, and the season started in February. The teams played 50 games. The Bulls only won 13 times. The five players with the most starts that season were Kukoc, Harper, Brown, Dickey Simpkins, and Brent Barry. Their roster was ridiculously poor. They averaged less than 82 points per game. I had gone from the penthouse to the outhouse.

In an attempt to maintain some relationship with the past, the Bulls forced Floyd to coach using the Triangle Offense, which Jackson had used to perfection. Tex Winter, the assistant coach who had created the offense and coached it with Jackson through all of those championship seasons, was kept on staff, but he did not have the same audience he once had.

The season ended on May 5, 1999, when the Bulls lost to the Orlando Magic at the United Center. At halftime of that game, the Bulls held a ceremony to fete Jackson, putting a special banner in the rafters to honor him. Jackson and Floyd said nice things about each other, and the baton was passed in some sort of official way.

A couple of weeks after the end of the season, the *Herald* changed my beat, making me a member of the Chicago Bears coverage team, and giving me the chance to pursue what has turned out to be a true love of mine, soccer, by making me cover the new Chicago Fire team in Major League Soccer. At the time, I did not know how to spell "soccer" but since then have coached the game, and watched hundreds of contests my children have played through the years.

After having "led" the Bulls to six titles, I was not surprised that I was able to push the Bears to the Super Bowl after the 2006 season (although they did not win the game). In 2008, I left the *Herald* to become a full-time freelancer, and in 2009 the NBA website NBA.com asked me to start covering the Bulls for them.

As of this writing, I have not been able to prod the Bulls to another title. Derrick Rose keeps getting hurt. But I am covering a coach in Tom Thibodeau who is almost as remarkable at his job as Phil Jackson was. I will not be surprised if Thibs and I are able to produce another title for the Chicago Bulls someday.

ACKNOWLEDGMENTS

Iwant to thank Triumph Books for asking me to write this book. I have never been one to spend much time in self-promotion (and I believe that has probably done me harm, at least in terms of making money) but from the day I got the job at the *Herald*, I have been asked to tell the stories about the time I spent with the Bulls. Now, they are all available to anyone who wants to hear them, and we don't have to depend on my memory.

I certainly want to thank the *Daily Herald* for hiring me in the first place. Its decision to go big-time in sports coverage changed the landscape of the newspaper business in Chicago. I was glad to be a part of it. I got to work for sports editors Jim Cook and Tom Quinlan, and their steady hand and light touch in terms of leadership made the entire experience a pleasure. There are times when I still can't believe I actually got to spend those 11 years traveling with the Bulls during the time of their greatest success.

Thank you to the players and coaches I dealt with, for their time and honesty and respectful behavior toward me. I was filled with trepidation about dealing with professional athletes the day I got the job, but it turned out to be a lot more pleasant than I thought.

Thanks also to the Bulls media relations staff, led by Tim Hallam and including Joyce Szymanski, John Diamond, Lori Flores Weiskopf, and Tom Smithburg. Thanks also to the press room staff at the Chicago Stadium and the United Center, led by Pam Kunkel, who predated me with the Bulls, is still working at the UC and still looks as young as she did the day I met her.

Lastly, and most importantly, thank you to my wife Janice. We got married in the fall of 1990 (which may have prompted the Bulls to win their first title that season), and for all those 11 years I was on the road a lot of the time. We started a family during those years, and a lot of responsibilities fell to her, even though she too was working.

The kids turned out magnificently, and for that, I cannot thank her enough.